Arts Administ

Second edition

John Pick

and

Malcolm Anderton

E & FN SPON
An Imprint of Chapman & Hall

London · Glasgow · Weinheim · New York · Tokyo · Melbourne · Madras

Published by E & FN Spon, an imprint of Chapman & Hall,
2–6 Boundary Row, London SE1 8HN, UK

Chapman & Hall, 2–6 Boundary Row, London SE1 8HN, UK

Blackie Academic & Professional, Wester Cleddens Road, Bishopbriggs, Glasgow G64 2NZ, UK

Chapman & Hall GmbH, Pappelallee 3, 69469 Weinheim, Germany

Chapman & Hall USA, 115 Fifth Avenue, New York, NY 10003, USA

Chapman & Hall Japan, ITP-Japan, Kyowa Building, 3F, 2-2-1 Hirakawacho, Chiyoda-ku, Tokyo 102, Japan

Chapman & Hall Australia, 102 Dodds Street, South Melbourne, Victoria 3205, Australia

Chapman & Hall India, R. Seshadri, 32 Second Main Road, CIT East, Madras 600 035, India

First edition 1980

Reprinted 1989, 1993

Second edition 1996

© 1980 J. Pick; 1996 John Pick and Malcolm Anderton

Typeset in Times, 10/10 by Saxon Graphics Ltd, Derby

Printed in Great Britain by St Edmundsbury Press, Bury St Edmunds, Suffolk

ISBN 0 419 18970 X

A catalogue record for this book is available from the British Library

Library of Congress Catalog Card Number: 95-74646

♾ Printed on permanent acid-free text paper, manufactured in accordance with ANSI/NISO Z39.48–1992 and ANSI/NISO Z39.48–1984 (Permanence of Paper).

To

Ann and Margaret

I don't want art for a few, any more than education for a few, or freedom for a few.

William Morris, *Arts and Crafts Movement*

Politics is the art of preventing people from taking part in affairs which properly concern them.

Paul Valéry, *Tel Quel*

Contents

Acknowledgements

The authors would like particularly to thank Dr Edwyn Anderton, Professor Anthony Field, Colin Berrisford, Keith Diggle, Professor Tony Watson, Geraldine Foreman, Peter Stark, J. Gordon Roebuck, Ian Watson, Professor Gurth Higgin, Peter F. Cresswell, Dr Steven Halls, Dr Eric Moody, Paul Scully, Dennis Howells, Michael Quine, Dr Caroline Gardiner, Rod Fisher, Bob Jones, Stewart Spencer, Mandy Middleton, Professor Joan Jeffri, Dr Michael Hammet, Robert Hutchison, Sir Kingsley Amis, Ian Robinson, Freda Steel, Mary Schwarz, Baz Kershaw, David Brierley, Gavin Henderson, Lord Rees Mogg, Dr Janet Summerton, Tom Higgins, David Easton, Dr John Elsom, Dr Robert Protherough, Ken Rowat, David Butler and Professor Simon Roodhouse, all of whom have at different times and in different ways informed and influenced the authors. We are grateful for the generous support of Gresham College for research which is mentioned here and will be fully reported in a later publication. Finally, for their encouragement and their forbearance, we owe a considerable debt to our publishers, and particularly to Amanda Killingback.

All names and details in the case studies have been invented for the purposes of this book, and do not relate to any particular person or organization. None of the persons acknowledged, nor quoted in the text, is responsible for any errors in the book. They, like the general arguments, are wholly the responsibility of the authors.

JP MA
1995

Introduction

This book is not a conventional text book, nor is it a conventional manual of management instruction. Yet the activity it is describing is of considerable, some would say supreme, importance. It is an activity undertaken in every country, all governments take a close interest in it, and its doings are frequently the subject of heated public debate. Its practitioners are also, as we shall see, bound by a common understanding of the nature of their work, and by a common ethical code. Yet arts administration is still not a profession, in any of the generally accepted senses of the term, and administering the arts well, though recognized as a highly specialized and skilled activity, still does not readily fit into any one academic category.

The nature of arts administration cannot be adequately described simply by offering the conventional description – 'arts administrators are people who administer the arts' – for, in spite of the recurrent use of the word 'administration' in this book, those who administer the arts are quite different from those who administer more conventional activities. The skills of arts administration are practised in a curious realm midway between artists, the arts and people, and are fuelled by an extraordinary and variable span of skills involving art, arts criticism, politics, psychology, information science, economics, sociology and education.

So, although there are skills which can effectively be learned from a text book, and some forms of administration and management that can effectively be learned from a manual, arts administration is not one of them. Effective arts administration depends above all on a deep knowledge of, and commitment to, art. Neither that, nor the highly variable balance of skills needed by practising arts administrators, can possibly be taught in one book. It would be fraudulent to pretend otherwise. *Arts Administration*, it is hoped, will be helpful to readers who already have some knowledge of, and commitment to, the administering of the arts, but it cannot stand instead of that knowledge, that commitment, or that practical experience.

Nor will a general book such as this completely satisfy professional economists or management experts, who may seek for detailed application of their disciplines in it, for although it describes the commonest parts of an arts administrator's work in some detail, and alludes to most of the other activities involved in arts administration, its descriptions must, inevitably, draw only fragmentarily from the vast literatures which exist on the relevant areas of cultural history, arts education, state arts funding, censorship and control, licensing, management, marketing and cultural economics. Moreover, the practices of the arts administrator are based on values extrinsic to their systems. As a result, much good arts administration, when surveyed by such outside experts, will seem confused, too much concerned with imprecise questions of human values rather than more tangible quantitative data.

So one uses the term 'arts administration' with some reluctance. In the last analysis it is useful only because it is the least defiled of the several terms which can be used to cover the activities of the person (or, more frequently nowadays, team of persons) making what we later define as the aesthetic contract between artists and their audiences. Arts administrators do not, in the narrowest sense of the term, spend much of their time administering – that is, creating and operating effective office routines. Nor do they spend substantial parts of their working day in any one of the conventional areas of management, although they frequently act, *inter alia*, as facility managers, personnel managers and resource managers. Nor can what they do be satisfactorily described as entrepreneurial, although arts administrators certainly act as innovators and animators. Yet of the available general titles for this work – managers, animators, agents, entrepreneurs, facilitators – 'administrator' remains, for our purposes, the most suitable term. Inevitably, it is more apt in some circumstances than others (English local authorities, for instance, give a different definition and status to the term 'administrator') and we are as a consequence persuasively redefining a term which is rarely used nowadays as a job title.

Arts administrators, then, are not conventional managers, animators, teachers, critics nor entrepreneurs, but a unique mixture of all of these. That uniqueness lies in the roles they adopt relative to the various legal, economic and state systems which bear upon them; their prime obligation is to a construct, 'art', which is neither product nor service, and whose demands may sometimes place them in opposition to prevailing political and legislative systems. As we later note, in our discussions of managerial roles, the arts administrator is frequently a maverick, whose authority and power derive from balancing many different pressures. The arts administrator is never a mere functionary, taking orders from state planners about the correct way to 'deliver' art.

To add to our difficulties, we have continuously to remind ourselves that the material with which the arts administrator works is neither a clearly delineated product, nor a simple service. 'Art' remains a notoriously cloudy and difficult term to define. Although there have in recent years been many attempts to describe the arts in terms of production line industry, arts administration is plainly different from managing a factory. Nor – in spite of the one British White Paper on the arts (1965), which seemed to be urging that the arts should thenceforward be seen as a free benefit for all, as education and health then were – is art the kind of service which can take its cue from people's 'needs'. People's 'needs' for the arts are of a different kind from their need to be educated, or from their need to be cured when they are ill. So it cannot be too often emphasized that in spite of attempts to treat them as one or the other, the arts are neither a service nor a range of products.

Moreover, it remains difficult to fit 'the arts' into modern political, economic or even philosophical theories. Indeed, even as a simple descriptive term 'the arts' covers a multitude of different constructs, created within vastly different media, which are understood by quite different means. In a scientific or technical sense, it is difficult to see the common bond between (for example) poetry, sculpture, radio drama, clowning and animation. So it is hardly surprising that politicians, economists and even many management experts, faced with the apparently vast differences between the various arts and faced with the equally extreme differences in the way they are administered, fall back upon describing the arts as an 'arts industry', and take refuge in attempting to describe the arts administrator's role as consisting simply in production line and budgetary management.

However seductive it may be – and however much easier it would make the writing of books such as this – any such approach evades all the difficult issues. By concentrating on economic values, it avoids asking why all societies put such high moral, spiritual and social value on the curious, irrational, compelling constructs of 'art'. Such an approach avoids confronting the awkward truth that artists shape the way we live, and the values we put upon human experience, much more than do economists or management theorists. The 'arts industry' – whether perceived as a production line or a service industry – is always a one-dimensional notion, and of limited application. In either sense the 'arts industry' has only a tangential relationship to the real arts world – the realms in which the various living arts meet their innumerable interrelated audiences.

The position taken by the authors of this book is that, in whatever kind of social context they may be working, and with whatever art form they may be concerned, the arts administrator's work always involves three essential and sequential steps:

- A deep knowledge of, and personal commitment to, chosen artist(s), art form or art forms.
- An equally full and imaginative understanding of the cultural history, awareness and other social conditions of all segments of the possible audience which may be reached by the chosen art(s).
- The ability, using every legitimate social, political and managerial skill, and with the fullest and most up-to-date political, legal and economic circumstances in mind, to forge the best available aesthetic contract, bringing together the arts and the largest and most appropriate audience in the best possible circumstances.

These steps will be borne in mind, and elaborated on, throughout the book. Meanwhile it is important to note that bad arts administration (what we later term 'arts bureaucracy') usually happens when this process occurs in reverse order – that is when some agency of social planning decides in a quantitative way that so much opera should be seen in a particular region, or that a certain number of books of poetry must be published in a certain year. The administrator then 'works backwards', finding 'art' which fits predetermined political or economic criteria, and the result is something without significant life or meaning. Notable examples of this 'bureaucratic art' were the gloomy murals of Lenin which used to be such a depressingly predictable feature of the cities of the old USSR, or (to make the point politically balanced) the murals that were produced throughout the USA during the Federal Arts Scheme of the early thirties, and which have now, like their Leninist counterparts, been thrown away and forgotten.

We must now make a further qualification. Although it does include description of the highly complicated system of state subsidy currently existing in Britain, together with a number of brief illustrations of systems in other countries, this book cannot claim to be complete, and – so rapidly does the system change – it is quite possible that some of the systems mentioned herein will have been modified by the time it is read and used. The time has long gone when it was possible to describe the 'British system' of state arts subsidy and to divide neatly the world of arts administration into 'public' and 'commercial' realms.

So, anyone imagining that they will here be able to read a complete account of the way Britain is being affected by European legislation, of the way the changing employment law relates to each separate part of the arts world, or the way each of the systems of state support for arts buildings, projects and organizations currently operates, and how they all interact, will be disappointed. However, enough information is given to enable the reader to understand, in broad terms, how things now stand. Some specific difficulties arts administrators are likely to face in the coming years are discussed in more detail, and others form the basis of the practical case studies at the end of this book. We also publish titles of reports, and addresses of organizations, from which up-to-date information can be gathered. In a word, although the principles on which this book is based do not change, the economic and legal contexts in which the arts administrator applies them are in constant agitation. As it would be wearisome to keep writing 'at the present time' in the text, the reader must be ready, where necessary, to bring his or her recent experience to bear upon the text, and, while retaining the general principles, modify and update some of the detail.

This is the best that can be done. For the arts administrator now works in a world of such flux, and so complicated in its parts, that no book could carry up-to-date information on every part of it, still less supply the necessary decoding and interpretation of all the new practices and policies. Books which have, in recent years, attempted to be simple and definitive about the way, for example, to staff and run a theatre, have found their work rapidly left behind by events.

Those that have attempted, more ambitiously, to describe 'the way things are going' in the arts have sometimes been left looking ridiculous, not least because artists have not created work which suited the developing management systems. This is an area where the practitioner needs to know as much about tradition and past practice (and the attendant successes and failures) as about present conditions, and needs always to know more about artists and their audiences than about current management practice. For even if someone were possessed of prodigious knowledge, perfectly understood each part of the system, and had outstanding managerial skill, it would not necessarily mean they were effective – unless they also had that dual empathy with art and with the public which is the prerequisite of the genuine arts administrator.

The last of these opening comments we have already touched upon. In many ways it is the simplest and, hopefully, most obvious point of all. The casual reader who has had little or no direct experience of arts administration might well wonder why there is so much history, and so much quibbling about definitions, in a book purporting to describe the present world of arts administration. Why not, it may be asked, simply describe the systems as they are, say what the arts administrator does, and be done with it?

Again, the answer to that lies in the nature of our subject. We are describing constructs and activities that vary in form from age to age, which have no meaning or significance by themselves, and which only acquire that significance when comprehended by the minds of readers, spectators or audiences. That comprehension does not take place in a void. Human beings do not place a value upon a painting, or a musical composition, or a poem, because they have within them an inbred calibrated set of mathematical responses. They recognize value in art because of the rich and accumulated response to life enshrined in their own language, and because of the myriad ways in which cultural history gives particular meanings to their experience, and to the art which illuminates it. To lay stress upon cultural history, and upon the language, is not then an academic indulgence. Cultural history and language is everything.

The bureaucrats, whom we have cast in the role of enemies to arts administration, will always try to describe art in quantitative terms – as a 'product' with economic characteristics, or as a 'service' with political ones – but if that language is adopted, art is essentially drained of its values. It becomes detached from the cultural history which nurtured it, and ultimately devoid of meaning. The bureaucrats' creation of a meaningless, glossy, highly purchasable art – the art which is a tool in 'cultural diplomacy', or the art which is used as an enticement in the 'tourist industry' – stands as the enemy of the kind of arts administration we wish to describe, and encourage, on these pages.

The changing British system

'Since 1939 much has changed in the way the arts have reached the public.' These much-quoted words began Evans and Glasgow's 1949 book, *The Arts in*

England, and it seems right to offer a variation of them here. For, since the first edition of *Arts Administration* was written some 15 years ago, much has changed in the political world, and in the economic assumptions which underlie it. The Thatcher/Reagan years brought a transformation of attitudes to the state and to management in general, and all of those things have, in the widest sense of the term, affected British culture. So it is just as true, even platitudinous, to begin this book by saying that, since 1979, very much more than between 1939 and 1949 has changed in the way the arts have reached the public.

In 1979 it was still possible to speak of the 'British system' of arts administration. The system referred to was operated on the 'arm's length principle', the belief that choices about the beneficiaries of state aid were best made by the great and the good, estimable members of society who were not its elected members and hence not immediately constrained by public opinion. Also in 1979 it was still generally agreed that the 'arm's length principle' was not effective if the great and the good were government stooges, but worked much better if the arm's length choices were made by members of the artists' peer group. Thus the 'arm's length principle' and 'peer group choice' went hand in hand.

In 1979, the received opinion was still that the Arts Council of Great Britain (as it then was) should be a reactive rather than a pro-active organization. The Council was there to react to local initiatives, or to respond to work artists chose to create. As Lord Keynes (1945) had said at the time of its foundation:

> ... everyone, I fancy, recognizes that the work of the artist in all its aspects is, of its nature, individual and free, undisciplined, unregimented, uncontrolled. The artist walks where the breath of the spirit blows him. He cannot be told his direction.

Although there were certainly signs in 1979 that the unfettered 'right to respond' would shortly be withdrawn from many of the world's arts councils (Pick, 1991; Pick, Anderton and Ajala, 1988), it was still thought when the first *Arts Administration* was published that the maintenance of the 'arm's length principle', together with 'peer group choice', guaranteed another principle which had been fought for, and grudgingly conceded by government, the freedom of the artist.

At the time of the creation of the Arts Council of Great Britain, it was generally agreed that, whatever happened, Britain would never have an arts ministry (Leventhal, 1990). With its ancient mistrust of state support of theatre and opera in France, most Britons now pointed with equal horror to what had happened in Mussolini's Fascist Italy, where 'Cars of Thespis' had taken state operatic and theatrical performances to every town and village in the country, and, it was said, the inhabitants had been compelled to attend them. Worse still was Hitler's Third Reich, where more than 8000 regional arts officers enforced a rigid discipline amongst publishers, exhibitors, theatrical producers and film makers.

British mistrust of that kind of centralized authority, and of any kind of prescriptive arts ministry, was no doubt made the greater by the dissemination, after the war, of the Nazi plans for the occupation of Britain. These ordinances of the German military authorities, entitled *German Occupied Great Britain*, had been written in 1941, and included plans to divide Britain into administrative regions, and within each one to ensure that:

All newspapers, pamphlets, publications, printed matter, reproductions obtained by mechanical or chemical methods, writings, pictures with or without words, music with words or explanations, or cinematograph films ... [*and*] all theatrical or cinematograph performances, pantomimes, readings, recitations, concerts, lectures or similar public performances of a nature to prejudice public order are forbidden.

Keynes' 1945 broadcast obviously tries to dampen fears that the new state intervention in the arts world might be a first step towards introducing such draconian measures in Britain. And although Keynes made a flattering reference to the USSR in that same broadcast, with the development of the cold war the Soviet Ministry of Culture was soon being cited as yet another example of the kind of government bureaucracy Britain abhorred.

Until the mid-seventies cultured opinion in Britain thus seemed to be united over two things. The first was that the state system must never become prescriptive, imposing unified standards on the whole country. In his 1945 broadcast Keynes had said:

How satisfactory it would be if different parts of the country would again walk their several ways as they once did and learn to develop something different from their neighbours and characteristic of themselves. Nothing can be more damaging than the excessive prestige of metropolitan standards and fashions.

While the 1965 White Paper had also urged, though more drably, that each of the provinces must 'have something of its own that is supreme in some particular field'.

The second belief was that in spite of its laid-back, reactive posture, state support was still much purer, more disinterested and generally superior to commercial or industrial support. Indeed the 1965 White Paper specifically warned against falling for the lure of commerce, insisting that the state could support artistic enterprise just as readily as the greedy moguls: 'There is no reason why attractive presentation should be left to those whose primary concern is with quantity and profitability.'

While as late as 1974/5 the secretary-general of the Arts Council of Great Britain (ACGB) was warning in his report against the encroachment of commerce in the Royal Opera House: 'Already many new productions are paid for by private or commercial sources. All this could mean our ceasing to have a Covent Garden which houses its own companies of opera and ballet among the best in the world.' That was almost the last cry of the purist supporters of exclusive state support for the arts. In the late seventies talk began of partnership between the state bodies, such as the arts councils, and the private and commercial sources, such as the Association for Business Sponsorship in the Arts (ABSA). Indeed the most obvious characteristic of arts funding in Britain in the eighties was the (state encouraged) growth of business sponsorship in the arts.

In the eighties arts councils were also urged (in Britain and elsewhere) to become 'businesslike', to drop their former reactive stance and become interventionist. They set up for the first time prescriptive three- and five-year plans for the arts which were, sometimes, eerily similar to prescriptive state plans on which (particularly when they had been produced in Nazi Germany, in Fascist Italy or in the Communist USSR) the British had formerly poured scorn.

Significantly, arts councils in their pronouncements increasingly adopted the language of commerce, forcing all who talked with them to see the arts as a commercial industry. For example, the 1986/7 Annual Report of the Arts Council of Great Britain referred to the arts directly as 'products' and audiences as 'consumers', and urged arts administrators to line up with 'current management practice', to 'minimize overheads' in the drive for 'productive efficiency', and to aim for 'optimum levels of production' of arts products with 'sales potential'. That kind of mercantile language had become so much a part of the ACGB, that the then secretary-general also felt no compunction in observing that 'the arts' were simply 'a successful part of Great Britain Plc'. Other organizations followed suit. In that same year the British Council announced in its annual report that accountability in a cultural organization came down to one thing: 'value for money'.

In 1992 the British Government created a Ministry for 'National Heritage' (DNH) – a somewhat amorphous term which seemed to include sport, the media and the press, the Royal Family, tourism, the old buildings that had previously been termed 'the heritage' – and the arts. Shortly after its inception it took responsibility also for the new National Lottery. In effect Britain now had the cultural ministry it had for so long affected to despise. And shortly afterwards, in 1994, the Arts Council of Great Britain was, without much ceremony, wound up.

However, the arts bureaucracy proved to be like Hydra's heads. Once one was removed, others sprang up to replace it. There are now four arts councils in Britain, with responsibilities respectively for England, Scotland, Wales and Northern Ireland. The former English arts associations have now become Regional Arts Boards (RABs), with their Board members selected and approved by the national arts council, and with considerable new responsibilities. For example, responsibility for all theatres except the major national ones has now passed to the new RABs, who have increased funds in order to meet their new responsibilities. Although this was presented as an act of 'devolution', the effective power in shaping policies and action remained at the centre, and the system became ever more tightly enmeshed. Thus most arts organizations applying for state aid in Britain had now to deal with a triple-tiered bureaucracy.

In 1979 one could say straightforwardly that local government was responsible for about half of public arts funding in Britain. The picture now is much more complicated. In the last fifteen years or so the structure of local government has been under constant review. Changes suggested by the most recent Boundary Commission (1995) have not been fully accepted by Parliament, and some parts of England and Wales are to be reviewed again. (In this drawn-out process some areas, such as Humberside, have experienced frequent changes, whilst London has been left without unified local government.) In that same period, available local authority finances have been sharply cut by central government, with the result that local authorities now have on average less than 2% of their total expenditure available for non-mandatory spending such as the support of the arts. In much of England the local authorities are more closely interlinked with the new RABs, and as a result local authority support of the arts can often be seen as interlinked with the support systems deriving from the Ministry.

One of the new Heritage Ministry's most contentious responsibilities is overall control of the new National Lottery. This, the first in Britain since 1826, began to function in 1994. The new Lottery is run by a private company, *Camelot*, appointed by the director-general of the National Lottery. After government taxation, a proportion of its profits are distributed equally between sport, charities, projects to mark the Millennium, heritage and the arts. Two new bodies, the National Lotteries Charity Board and the Millennium Commission, oversee distribution to charities and the Millennium Fund, while distribution to the arts and heritage is the responsibility of units in the Arts Council of England and the National Heritage Memorial Fund respectively. Thus, the distribution of the new lottery's profits is also intertwined with the triple-layered arts bureaucracy. The new lottery is not a new and separate source of funding, but an extension of the existing state-controlled funding system.

The outer reaches of that increasingly complex, and increasingly interrelated, system tended to show the same characteristics – a growing bureaucratization, coupled with a move away from their former 'reactive' stance. The Crafts Council and the British Council were moved under the general umbrella of the new Heritage Ministry. Both were exhaustively reorganized, and both produced prescriptive 'strategies' for their respective fields. Long-standing funding agencies such as English Heritage also suffered drastic reorganization. Many new strategic plans ambitiously straddled the former public and private sectors. Meanwhile bodies like the Gulbenkian Foundation, or the new Foundation for Sport and the Arts, were often seriously affected by the enlarging activities of the new Heritage Ministry, even though they were not a part of it. Indeed the latter foundation, which was largely funded by the football pools promoters, found its funds sharply cut in 1995 when the impact of the new state lottery on spending on the football pools became apparent.

In addition, although the degree of its commitment and membership remained a contentious issue, in effect Britain had become a full member of the European Union. One result was that in the late eighties development projects, in particular those involving renovation of arts buildings and urban precincts, drew heavily on newly available European funding sources. These systems are complex, but have been well explained by Fisher (1992). Britain has been a major beneficiary of the European Regional Development Fund in particular. Theatres that have been assisted towards renovation by substantial grants include the Theatre Royal, Newcastle (£3.4 million); the Alhambra Theatre, Bradford (£2.12 million) and the Grand Theatre, Swansea (£2.7 million). Smaller but significant sums from the European Social Fund have also grant-aided other projects; for example the North East Media Training Centre in Gateshead in 1989 received a grant of £260 000.

Those European sources also became interlocked with the growing state arts bureaucracy, and the overall result has been greatly to increase the degree of central state control of all the major art forms in Britain. Some critics would say it is no less menacing for being genteelly applied: for example, by allocating funds only to applicants who have taken care to form themselves in the prescribed state image, and who prudently discuss their aims and objectives in the fashionable new commercial arts language – a language which is, as we have said, a further instrument of control.

The way the British Arts Council has exercised control over the visual arts, has been described by Moody (1994):

In 1993 an apparently radical transformation of the system with wholesale devolution precipitated by another horticultural metaphor, 'The Glory of the Garden' (Arts Council, 1985) has not materialised. A review of the structure and management of the system (Wilding, 1989) and a review of the council itself (Price Waterhouse Assocs., 1993) and not to mention the 'consultative process' leading to a Creative Future have not encouraged an examination of the efficiency of the curatorial orthodoxy (as repre-sented by the Hayward and Serpentine Galleries) to achieve the object of the system. Devolution of direct control of the two galleries has been achieved by making them revenue clients of the Arts Council and trans-ferring exhibition staff, including the director of the department, from the Council. A belated campaign of regional development transferring some of the 'eleven independent organizations' to the care of the Regional Arts Boards and encouraging local authority art museums to put on programmes of contemporary art exhibitions has been tightly controlled by the renamed Visual Arts Department. The mechanism of dispensing exhibition project funding to favoured curators ... developing curatorial cloning by Arts Council traineeships and, last year, a new course in cura-torship with the close involvement of the department are efficient mecha-nisms for retaining control.

Meanwhile the state itself, despite much talk of rolling back its frontiers, curiously seemed to grow in size and power. In 1910 the British state directly employed only 55 000 people, and was responsible for the expenditure of 2½p in the pound. By 1979 it employed some 730 000, and was responsible for 60p in every pound spent.

After 1979 there was some reduction in direct government employment and spending, but this was counterbalanced by a corresponding increase in 'non-departmental bodies', sometimes called quangos (Quasi Autonomous National Governmental Organizations), bodies aiming to achieve various publicly desirable ends, which are set up by government but not a direct part of it. The arts councils, Museum Association and the British Tourist Board all fall within this category. In 1979 quangos were responsible for spending some £13.9 million. By 1993 they were responsible for spending more than £2 billion – their spending power had thus multiplied by 145. When such indirect government spending is added to direct expenditure, it is seen that the government still spends, directly or indirectly through the quangos, some 65p in every pound.

For the arts administrator then, the last fifteen years or so have seen a growth in the number of bureaucratic cells involved in the state licensing and funding systems, coupled with a great increase in the way they relate and interact. There has also been an unprecedented amount of legislation in other fields, such as employment law, education, public transport and social services, which bears heavily upon the arts administrator's work, and with which the arts administrator must deal. So to administer the arts successfully now requires quite

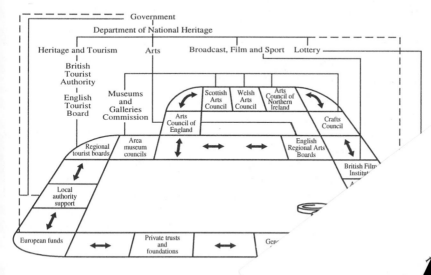

Figure 1 The arts administration board: 35 000 play
direction

astonishing legerdemain, an ability to move on the 'arts administration board' (Figure 1) with great fluency, and, it must be said, the ability to outwit and outmanoeuvre the deadly plans of the worst of the arts bureaucrats.

Equal vigilance is needed to counter the more insidious effects of the stifling commercial language, which is nowadays used even by people who would claim to be friends of the arts. Here, for example, is a paragraph from an Arts Council pamphlet called *The Arts: a Great British Success Story* (1986):

> The arts have been one of our greatest success stories – perhaps the greatest. We are asking the nation to invest in this well-proved product, to provide the cash to ensure that past glories do not become insubstantial memories, and that present achievements can be built upon for even greater returns in the future.

The insidious slide from talking of the perfectly genuine 'past glories' of British art to discussing the greater 'returns' hoped for in the future, or the way in which 'the arts' are reduced to becoming a 'well-proved product', is easily seen on the printed page. But the arts administrator will find it harder when all those around speak and write like this. To take another, more recent, example, from the *Arts Tourism Marketing Handbook* (1994):

> The term 'arts' covers a multitude of activities, including theatre – from mime, street theatre and puppetry to circuses; dance – from classical and contemporary ballet to other contemporary and folk dance; classical and other types of music such as jazz, rock and soul; opera, art galleries, museums and public art; film and video; and literature. Add recording, broadcasting and publishing and, using the widest definition of the arts, you have a major industry which has an annual turnover of £10 billion, accounts for 2.5 per cent of consumer spending and 1.28 per cent of GDP, employs over 2 per cent of the working population, generates £4 billion in overseas earnings – and is a major attraction for British and overseas visitors.

In such a piece it is noteworthy that although the arts are introduced as 'activities', they are soon being described as an industry, with statistics about 'employment' and 'overseas earnings' being offered to justify their importance. The author does not, for instance, show any interest in the **activity** of reading, but only in publishing – a 'production industry' which can readily be described in terms of 'turnover' and 'consumer spending'. It is the purchase of books which is deemed to be significant, not what is read, nor whether reading the book gives pleasure and benefit. The value of the 'activity' is presumed to follow, self-evidently, from the economic data.

This kind of oppressive commercial language has been a characteristic of ch that has been written or said about the arts during the last fifteen years. It rs still, particularly in some of the pronouncements made about 'training' ministrators. No doubt other, equally insidious, attempts will be made to colour and distort the traditions and practices of arts administration, and they in their turn must be resisted. The constant vigilance the arts administrator needs is strengthened (much as a priest's is strengthened by constant reference to basic theology) by constant reference to cultural history, coupled with adherence to the three principles of arts administration that we outlined above.

The sense of isolation the arts administrator, or team of arts administrators, will nowadays feel, inevitably grows as bureaucrats seek to standardize practice (thereby putting emphasis on every part of administrative practice except what is at its centre: the quality of art, and the relationship it makes with its audience), and seek to use every system of control to impose their will. When the DNH in 1994 announced it was seeking 'increasing efficiency and effectiveness' from local government it openly stated that it would use 'a number of mechanisms' to get its way. These included standardized 'service level agreements' for all arts facilities run by local authorities, general imposition of the Audit Commission's 'performance indicators', and 'the establishment of mechanisms' for effective consumer feedback. The arts administrator, concerned as he or she must be with aesthetic contracts more local and more singular than could possibly be covered by nationally-imposed notions of standardized practice, must be ready to oppose such oppressive moves where they impinge upon art, the freedom of artists and the right of people to ignore imposed criteria of judgement, and instead to make their own, unique, responses.

The changing audience

During the eighties there was a belief, particularly in the United States but also in Britain, in the efficacy of 'trickle down economics', the belief that if the successful businessmen and entrepreneurs were well rewarded, the benefits of the patronage and spending of the rich, and the further employment their largesse generated, would trickle down through the economy to everyone's benefit. An important condition of all this was that there should be general low taxation, and that there should be no punitive taxation on the rich.

The trickle down economics of the Reagan/Thatcher years did not in fact appear to produce the general benefits that were expected. A 1995 report from the Joseph Rowntree Foundation pointed out that in Britain, inequality of income had rapidly increased since the late 1970s. Whereas between 1966 and 1977 all wages grew at much the same rate, after 1978 benefits from economic growth were unevenly distributed. High wages grew in the period 1979–92 by 50%, median wages by 35%, whilst wages for the lowest-paid hardly changed at all.

The problem of how to give access to the arts for the poorer and least advantaged sections of society was thus even greater in the early nineties than it had been in 1979. And there were other newly disadvantaged groups. Great emphasis had been laid on the development of Britain's run-down inner cities, and there had been some spectacular successes, notably in Birmingham and

Glasgow. Indeed during the eighties city development was a particular feature of the newly-defined 'Europe' (Biachini and Parkinson, 1993). Yet this was achieved in Britain at some cultural cost both to the smaller market towns, and to the rural population in general. Another feature of the last fifteen years has thus been the increasing disenfranchisement of the rural population, who have witnessed an increasing concentration of cultural resources in urban areas, coupled with a decline in rural transport systems, and a steady erosion of valuable facilities such as country schools, village shops, post offices and travelling library services.

Perhaps more important still has been the gradually increasing lack of interest, in bureaucrats' plans, in the genuine response of the public. Overall, the general public has been downgraded in significance. Arts bureaucrats in Britain will now quite openly say that it is they, the bureaucrats, who are deciding 'audience priorities'. Local authorities, as we have seen, are being urged to impose standardized criteria for 'effective consumer representation and feedback'. Increasingly the trend is for bureaucrats to determine what is art, and to prejudge and to standardize what the public response 'ought' to be.

Conversely, and this may even be thought menacing in its implications, those popular arts and entertainments which make an immediate contact with large audiences are subject to increasingly restrictive legislation. *The Criminal Justice and Public Order Act 1994* (whose effects are discussed in greater detail later) empowers the state authorities to raid popular musical festivals, to close them immediately, confiscate all equipment and to order anyone they choose who is within five miles of the event to leave the area (Sections 63, 64, 65). Yet the promotion of a different kind of music, which has been approved of and given the epithet 'art' by the arts bureaucracy, and which is a 'priority' in 'audience development' will be given every assistance, including financial aid, by the same authorities. All of which would matter much less if one could be absolutely sure that the difference between the music played at a rave or rock concert and the music played at a subsidized new music concert was simply a difference between the bad and the good.

One cannot be sure. So the arts administrator now often has a lonely and unenviable task, that of standing by individual judgements in opposition to those of the bureaucratic juggernaut.

REFERENCES

ACGB (1986) *The Arts: A Great British Success Story.*
Arts Council of Great Britain (ACGB) *Annual Reports* 1974/5 and 1986/7.
Berlin (1941) *Operational Instructions for the Administration of Occupied Britain.*
Biachini, F. and Parkinson, M. (eds) (1993) *Cultural Policy and Urban Regeneration: The West European Experience.*
British Council *Annual Reports* 1985/6 and 1986/7.

English Tourist Board (ETB) (1994) *Arts Tourism Marketing Handbook.*

Evans, I. and Glasgow, M. (1949) *The Arts in England.*

Fisher, R. (1992) *Who Does What in Europe.*

HMSO (1965) *The Arts: The First Steps.*

Joseph Rowntree Foundation (1995) *Wealth and Inequality in Britain.*

Keynes, M. (1945) *The Arts Council: Its Policy and Hopes.*

Leventhal, F.M. (1990) 'The best for the most', in *Twentieth Century British History*, Vol. 1, No. 3.

Moody, E. (1994) 'The failure of State support for the visual arts in Britain', in *Cultural Policy* (ed. O. Bennet), Vol. 1, No. 1.

Pick, J. (1991) *Vile Jelly: The Birth, Life and Death of the Arts Council of Great Britain.*

Pick, J., Anderton, M. and Ajala, R. (1988) *The Arts in a State.*

The arts

1.1 THE ARTS ADMINISTRATOR AND ART

The arts administrator aims to create an **aesthetic contract** between an artist and an audience in such a way that the largest possible number of people receive the maximum pleasure and benefit from the art. At different times, and within the different arts, this contract may be created in a variety of ways: by promoting club entertainment, by setting up and advertising a performance in a publicly licensed building, by broadcasting into people's homes, by publishing a book, selling a CD, making a community video, busking, presenting a concert on a public bandstand, by erecting a public sculpture, painting a mural, producing a street event, by teaching an evening class, or by dozens of other means. Only in totalitarian states does art reach its public solely by means of specially designated culture houses and the like. Even then, within such societies there is often an arts underground disseminating the forbidden arts.

In more open democracies the arts may reach their public in parks, private homes, on sea and in the air, in shopping arcades and churches, as well as through arts centres, concert halls, galleries and other designated arts venues. Though arts administrators frequently work to promote a particular venue, they must always bear in mind that the significant contact between artist and audience does not take place wholly in the building where the right to enjoy it was purchased, and it may take place (as with the purchase from a bookshop of a book of poetry) wholly outside it.

Even in the performing arts, good arts administration cannot be measured solely by ticket sales. After all, the performance may not have been worth putting on. Or the audience may not make contact with the performed work at all (they may, as jet-lagged tourist audiences are supposed to do, fall asleep). Or, sometimes, members of an audience may only come fully to understand and enjoy the work much later. Surprising artistic experiences can come to us all by our own firesides, out walking, or waiting for a bus.

Art may be said fully to exist, not from the moment of its creation or re-creation or from the moment that it is sold, but from the time it is understood by and gives benefit to its participants or audience. ('Audience' in this context also refers to 'viewers', 'onlookers', 'readers', 'listeners' and other beneficiaries of the arts.) That understanding may be partial, the benefit may be blurred, and a work may be received with controversy rather than with unanimous acclaim, but the essential point to make is that a work of art is not truly born until it has been received by the public. Thus the arts administrator's work takes place essentially in the public realm, and involves a delicate perception of whether **this** art may be understood and give benefit to or even be tolerated by **that** audience (which we later term an art work's 'proper' audience). This involves a dual empathy with audience and artist, a unique sympathetic and imaginative skill which lies at the heart of every arts administrator's work.

Thus, an arts administrator must always concentrate as much as possible upon the art itself, and the aesthetic contract with the audience which gives it life and meaning. A politician or (taking the definition we offered in the Introduction) an arts bureaucrat may wish to divert the administrator's attention elsewhere: to the production costs, or sales figures perhaps. These things are important, and the arts administrator must be fully inward with them, but such quantitative data cannot be the final measure of the administrator's work. A full house of bored people watching a bad play is nearly as bad as a good play performed to an empty house.

There have, of course, always been pressures upon the administrator to consider the arts only as goods to be sold, and to ignore that necessary and over-riding empathy with both audience and artist that we noted above. There will always be siren voices urging arts administrators to ignore the cultural traditions within which they work, to forget the longer-term needs of artist and audience, and to concentrate instead upon getting good (short-term) 'business' results. Not infrequently, such advocates quote a dictum attributed to the great British actor Sir Henry Irving: 'The drama must succeed as a business, or it will fail as an art.'

In fact that is a slight but significant misunderstanding, for, in that context, 'business' had a different meaning. Irving was objecting to 'reformers' (with aims extrinsic to the drama) intruding into the day-to-day business of theatre. By 'business' he was referring not to trade, but to a wider notion of profession-alism. His point was that theatre had to maintain its traditions, its wide popular appeal, and be subject to the lively criticism of its own audiences, or it did not deserve the term 'art'. The actual paragraph, from an address given in Edinburgh in 1881, runs:

And so I would say of what we sometimes hear so much about – dramatic reform. It is not needed; or, if it is, all the reform that is wanted will be best effected by the operation of public opinion upon the administration of a good theatre. That is the true reforming agency, with this great advantage, that reforms which come by public opinion are sure, while those which come without public opinion cannot be relied upon. The dramatic reformers are very well-meaning people. They show great enthusiasm. They are new converts to the theatre, most of them, and they have the zeal of converts. But it is scarcely according to knowledge. These ladies and gentlemen have scarcely studied the conditions of theatrical enterprise, which must be carried on as a business, or it will fail as an art. It is an unwelcome, if not an unwarrantable intrusion to come among our people with elaborate advice, and endeavour to make them live after different fashions than those which are suitable to them, and it will be quite hopeless to attempt to induce the general body of a purely artistic class to make louder and more fussy professions of virtue and religion than other people. In fact it is a downright insult to the dramatic profession to exact or to expect any such thing.

By 'all the reform that is wanted will be best effected by the operation of public opinion upon the administration of a good theatre', Irving was rightly setting the highest standards for the administrators of his own time. A base for those high standards was the immediacy of contact between artist and audience.

That contact is now much harder to achieve, partly because state funding systems frequently commission artists' work, and that work is not infrequently described as art as soon as state aid is promised to it. Here, for example, is the Arts Council of Great Britain describing one of the 'major achievements' in the art of the previous year in its 1985/6 Annual Report:

> Following a unique feasibility study commissioned by the Arts Council, leading sculptors nationwide were invited to submit designs for a new landmark in Holbeck Triangle, Leeds, a piece of waste land between the railway lines leading into the City Station. With backing from the Arts Council, British Rail, Leeds City Council and arts groups in Yorkshire, sculptor Anthony Gormley was commissioned to produce the special large scale work which will give travellers a dramatic first impression of the city.

The work is accorded the status of art by the fact that the Arts Council commissioned the 'feasibility study', and by the prestige of the sponsors. In describing it as one of the year's artistic successes, the Arts Council also prescribes the effect it will have on its public, giving 'a dramatic first impression' of Leeds. It is thus an example of a phenomenon which has become much more common in the last fifteen years, bureaucratically-defined art. For its 'success' existed only in the minds of the planners. It was never actually constructed. It was never placed in Holbeck Triangle, and no member of the public had any kind of reaction to it, dramatic or otherwise.

For the novelist Kingsley Amis (1989) the licence given to the bureaucrat to define art is a fundamental objection to the British system of arts funding:

The way an artist is paid profoundly affects his product. At one extreme he sells what he has already made, at the other he is paid in full before he starts making anything – that is he is commissioned, he is paid in advance. It is this second mode of payment that goes to the recipient of state subsidies. An artist in that position is relieved of the pressure to please the public, the audience, and is free to court the approval of an inner circle of colleagues, critics and experts to be self-indulgent. One quotation summarises a large part of it. Arnold Schoenberg, who started atonal composition in 1908: 'I believe that a real composer writes for no other purpose than to please himself. Those who write because they want to please others, who have audiences in mind, are not real artists'.

Yet, even if some art and some arts activities are given in advance a kind of benediction by arts bureaucrats, it is still the arts administrator's duty to create the circumstances in which as many people as possible may draw the maximum pleasure and benefit from it. The arts administrator must strive to bring the work beneficially into contact with the largest possible audience so that it may genuinely earn its title as an art.

The arts administrator will also be keenly aware that all art is constantly being revalued. Public reaction varies from age to age, even from year to year, and there is no single moment when a work of art finds its perfect audience and enters the divine canon of art for all eternity. Yet, no art is fully born until it has an audience. A poem is not a poem until it has readers, nor does a play (usually) exist until it is performed. However muted, confused or variable reactions may be, the audience is an integral part of the creation of art.

The curtain had barely risen in May 1913 at the Théâtre des Champs-Élysées in Paris on Diaghilev's *The Rite of Spring* when the catcalling began, drowning the orchestra so that the dancers could hardly hear Stravinsky's score. The more conservative members of the audience booed, while intellectual cadres shouted in support. At the end of the performance the police had to be called to restore order. Yet, despite that unruly reception, an art work had been born, though its baptism was not to take place fully until the Joffrey Ballet's reconstruction of 1987, and the ballet's second Paris performance, seventy-eight years after the first, in 1991.

1.2 WHAT ARE THE ARTS? THE BRITISH EXAMPLE

Although to many people the question will seem pedantic, the arts administrator must from the first be clear about what he or she sees as the parameters of 'the arts'. After all, people draw pleasure and benefit from many activities which would not be considered as art (and sometimes conspicuously fail to draw benefit or pleasure from things experts term 'art'). So we must ask again, what are 'the arts'? Certainly, the constructs and activities referred to by the term differ markedly between countries: the circus is an honoured, state-financed art in

Russia and China, whereas in Britain traditional circus is all but outlawed, and certainly receives little or no state money. Within Britain, the dividing line between art and non-art is unclear. One can still start an argument by asking any group to discuss whether, say, jazz, photography, rap poetry and graffiti are 'art' or not.

The question becomes more complicated still when we look at the history of the term in English. Until the middle part of the nineteenth century 'art' was a descriptive term, referring to any activity which gave pleasure or benefit, and which involved a degree of skill. Thus Byron could refer to the 'arts of war and peace'; Jane Austen to the 'arts' of letter-writing and conversation. More earthily, Johnson could say that any man who exposed himself while drinking 'hath not the art of getting drunk'. The arts were pursued domestically as readily as in public places, and public gatherings for the appreciation of art were likely to be promoted by 'societies' of local amateurs interested in music, art or scientific debate (Harrison, 1984), or by the many commercial showmen who played the small theatre 'circuits', or toured with fit-up booths to the traditional fairs and carnival dates.

It is true that a distinction was sometimes made between the arts which were thought to be 'improving' and activities which were thought to be morally corrupting. There was for instance considerable establishment hostility to popular entertainments in Britain in the eighteenth and early nineteenth centuries (Malcolmson, 1973). But the perceived threat from different pleasures and pastimes fluctuated from decade to decade, between different political and religious forums. A popular print of about 1800 showed a series of pure arts leading upwards to heaven, and a series of impure ones leading down to the flames of hell. Amongst the improving arts were gardening, dancing, needlework and cooking, whilst stages on the road to perdition included novel reading and going to the theatre. Yet a century later serious drama was held to be 'improving' while dancing had dubious associations – the ballet for example could only be seen as a brief intermission in variety theatres, while dances such as the waltz were held by some to be immoral, and 'unsuitable for young ladies'. (Gardening had ceased to be considered as an art at all.)

'The arts' ceased to be so loosely defined in the second half of the century. A prime cause was the *Ten Hours Act*, 1847, which increased the non-working time available to most people. So, from the middle of the century, leisure, which had been made a meaningful commodity for city dwellers by the factory shift systems, soon became also a desirable commodity (Thompson, 1980). For those living in the countryside, leisure could still be enjoyed casually, often without payment, as entries from the Rev. Kilvert's *Diary* (1870) suggest:

16th. June. We walked up through the town to the Hand Hotel, stopping a moment on the fine quaint old grey stone bridge of Dee with its sharp angled recesses, to look down into the clear rocky swift winding river, so like the Wye. As we came near the Hand, we heard the strains of a Welsh harp, the first I ever heard. The harper was playing in the hall the air 'Jenny Jones'. ... He was a beautiful performer and he was playing on a handsome harp of sycamore and ash, which he had won as a prize in an Eisteddfod. I had a good deal of talk with him after he had done playing. He told me there were very few people now who could play the Welsh harp, and the instrument was fast going out of use. The young people learn the English harp which is much easier being double stringed instead of treble stringed. The Welsh harp has no silver string and it is played from the left shoulder while the English harp is played from the right shoulder.

When a near contemporary of Kilvert, James Harker, set up a village concert in a Leicestershire village, there was still a surprising variety of talent available in a rural backwater, but Harker (writing about the year 1850) has a more obviously commercial approach:

One Dear Old Friend, the first man I ever spoke to in Oadby, and one I shall never Forget, was John Newnham who Lived Next Door. He was so courteous and quiet and would try to Please every one. He would sometimes, like other Men, enjoy himself but I Have never seen him out of Temper. He was a very Tall Man, with no flesh on his bones and he looked as Hard as Nails. He was a Singer at the Church and out of Church he was a High Kicker. Very Few men was Better than him. I once se him knock a Pipe off the tall mantle shelf in the White Horse Tap Room.

He once said He would make me a Good Singer and he tried to learn me Notes, but my Head was too Thick. I think Has he did that i Contained Singing material, but was unable to Cultivate it.

One day he suggested that we got up an Entertainment. This is the Programme:

John Newnham,	High Kicker
Joseph Ditto,	Singer
Mrs Holyoake,	Violen
Thos. Ditto,	Acrobat
Thos. Norman,	Violen,
James Colver,	Banjo
Me,	on the bones
William Colver,	Stump Oration.

We wanted Johnnie Matthews and Minnie but Failed to get them.

We hired a Room at the Pub on the Left Hand Side and charged threepence Admission. When the time arrived we was in the Best of Form and we all knew it would be a Great Success. Who knows, we thought, there might be a Great Future for some of us.

Meanwhile urban workers fought, with gradual success, both for better wages and for more free time. Soon the fast growing cities of Britain contained tens of thousands of people who, for the first time, had some money to spend, a little leisure to spend it in, a growing transport infrastructure which could carry them to entertainment venues in and around their cities, and (increasingly) an education sufficient to enable them to read the advertisements which, quite rapidly, had become a major shaping force in people's lives (Williams, 1980).

The entertainments which could be purchased in the cities were hardly less rough than country entertainments, but were presented by much more mercenary promoters. The atmosphere in the common music halls, pleasure gardens and minor theatres was simple and rough, as we are reminded when reading Mrs Bancroft's (1888) account of her visit twenty-nine years earlier to a theatre off London's Tottenham Court Road, that she intended later to buy:

> Some of the occupants of the stalls (the price of admission was, I think, a shilling) were engaged in devouring oranges (their faces being buried in them) and drinking ginger-beer. Babies were being rocked to sleep, or smacked to be quiet, which proceeding, in many cases, had the opposite effect! A woman looked up to our box, and seeing us staring aghast with, I suppose, an expression of horror on my face, first of all 'took a sight' at us, and then shouted, 'Now then, you three stuck-up ones, come out o' that, or I'll send this 'ere orange at your 'eds.

Performing arts venues were habitually used for public meetings by Chartists, the republican agitators and, later, the suffragettes. Looking to events in France, the British authorities began to see the theatres and the halls as the meeting places of a potential revolution, and a serious battle, political, educational and economic, was joined for the country's leisure time. No longer could the powers that be, worried by the vast and potentially disruptive populations that were gathered in the new cities, benignly accept that domestic pastimes, the vernacular arts, commercial entertainments, amateur societies, and local government arts amenities all had equal status on the same cultural map. They had to define the 'higher' arts clearly, so that people could be moulded and improved by them. Equally, people must be warned against and steered away from what the authorities considered the more dangerous and even revolutionary effects of the 'lower' arts.

Towards the end of the century 'the arts' began to shift from being a descriptive term to being a judgemental one. As Williams (1976) pointed out, 'artist' was by then being used in a new and special sense, and 'the arts' were now validated, not by the general will, but by the approval of high society, often given by the creation of a new 'Royal Academy' for that art form, combined with recognition within the rapidly growing new education system.

This new judgement of the division within the arts had two important consequences. It relegated many traditional pleasures, not included in the state's new educational curricula as 'art', to lesser status. Thus Britain's long traditions in cartooning, folk dance, the work song and woodcarving (to choose at random from a long list) were now thought of as 'lower arts'. A second consequence was that some arts had to modify their nature and their organization in order to be placed on the 'high arts' list. This was particularly true of the serious drama, which had to distance itself from the raffish encumbrances of music hall, pantomime and popular melodrama before it made the cut.

Even from so cursory a description, it will be seen that Britain's 'culture gap' (Hall, 1984) has a long history. It existed before the two World Wars, the growth of the media, mass unemployment, mass tourism or any of the other twentieth century causes which have been blamed for it – though each in turn has affected its nature. It existed well before financial support for the arts in Britain was fully systematized in the creation of the Arts Council of Great Britain in 1945.

Despite being in a more spasmodic and fragmentary form, financial intervention by the state had been a factor both in the creation of the 'culture gap' and in attempts to close it. The British government had intervened in arts economies from the middle of the eighteenth century: occasionally offering special grants for the purchase of art collections, state pensions for artists, state support for cultural festivals, and government grants for the repair of the Covent Garden opera house. In the First World War, with the Garrison Theatres network, there had even existed the nucleus of a state arts funding system, though far smaller than the systems which developed between 1939 and 1945 (Hewison, 1981). There had also been a number of national lotteries to benefit the arts since Queen Elizabeth I first organized one in 1577, selling 45 000 tickets at ten shillings each and offering as prizes 'plate and certaine sortes of merchaundise'.

Most importantly, there had, since the middle of the nineteenth century, been increasing support for the arts from the new local governments which had grown up rapidly following the decisive *Municipal Reform Act* of 1835. The growth of Britain's vast network of museums and municipal art galleries, to say nothing of its impressive local library system, was almost entirely due to local government support. Local authority resorts played an equally important part in the growth of Britain's orchestras and bands at the turn of the century.

The private sector was, then, a much larger patron of the arts than national and local government combined. Nearly all the theatres built in nineteenth century Britain, together with many of its concert halls, were paid for either by philanthropic industrialists or by private speculators looking for profit. 'Industrial sponsorship' thus occupied a much larger segment of the arts economy a century ago than it does today. Moreover, many museums, galleries and local halls were built and run directly as a result of cooperation between the new local government authorities and private funds. In nearly every city and major town during the nineteenth century state and private patronage worked smoothly together (Pick and Anderton, 1990). Even if the cultural map of late nineteenth century England were to be pictured solely as an 'arts industry' in the modern fashion, it would still be more impressive than today's. A century ago, when England's population was some 29 000 000, it contained around 450 museums and galleries, and 1300 other licensed places of amusement. It was calculated at that time (in the 1892 *Theatres Report*) that the performing arts in England alone employed 350 000 people and had a capital of more than £6 000 000.

However, in both the private and the government sectors, the division between 'higher' and 'lower' arts was growing – a division made by an authority partly vested in the powerful educational forums, partly in the still authoritative religious bodies, and partly in the metropolitan establishment. It was a division which cut across art forms, and was reinforced by civic legislation. New museums and galleries were considered to be on a more elevated plane than the shows of Britain's travelling showmen; the theatre formed into the divisions anticipated by the 1843 *Theatres Act* with the serious drama anxious to prove itself as 'art', and the fit-ups, music halls, sensational melodramas, burlesques and pantomimes now considered mere entertainment; the 'Italian' opera was being transmuted into the national opera, with the English Opera movement paradoxically relegated to the second rank. In the arts, no less than elsewhere, the country divided: the galleryite in the music halls inhabited totally different realms from the swell in the West End stall.

Imperceptibly the 'higher arts', with their avant-garde movements and their highly educated and sophisticated followers, came to seem the property of the fashionable city world and became most closely associated with those who had the most opportunity, leisure, spending power and education to enjoy them – that is, the middle-class town and city dwellers.

It was inevitable that most efforts to provide the 'higher' arts had been made in centres of the densest population, and, equally inevitably, those urban concentrations of art were widely promoted as being superior to the more ancient arts of the countryside or the raffish promotions of the travelling show-men. The arts were already associated with the rich city dwellers, and, in addition, were now becoming (most notably in the great International Trade Fairs that were a feature of the turn of the century) the currency of cultural diplomacy between rich and powerful states. 'High art' was becoming more international, and less rooted in regional and local cultures. By the end of the century the die was effectively cast. Writing of the collapse of the gentle rural traditions in his part of rural Berkshire, the Rev. M.J. Bacon wrote in 1894: 'But all these things are relics of a past age now. Shins are tenderer, mouths less wide, or at least the dialect is less broad; and the certificated schoolmaster and the railways have done their deadly work.' Bacon is perhaps unnecessarily pessimistic; local and regional art, amateur work, rural crafts, the folk traditions of song, dance and storytelling have been resilient, as have local dialects. But they have too often been excluded from consideration by those who seek to mould our culture because of such persuasive redefinition of the term 'the arts'. That has meant that the whole of the rest of British culture, placed behind a battery of slightly condescending terms: 'pastimes', 'hobbies', 'entertainment', 'heritage', 'leisure' and 'recreation' among them, including activities once thought to be art, or which have all or most of the characteristics of art, is relegated to the grey and inferior status of popular amusement.

When the Arts Council of Great Britain was created in 1945, therefore, it was neither the first intervention by the state in the world of the arts, nor a survey of an undifferentiated age of arts activities. It had no *tabula rasa* on which to write. For, in the manner we have broadly indicated, British culture and the arts had already been segmented, with a value system strongly suggesting a permanent artistic hierarchy. So, virtually from the start, and despite the much broader initial vision suggested by the Arts Council's first chairman (Keynes, 1945), the Arts Council effectively espoused the (by then) well-established notions of the superior 'higher arts'. Its remit excluded commercial showmanship, the folk arts and the bucolic traditions of rural Britain, crafts, the amateur arts, the media and of course all religious ceremony. Thus, the definition of 'the arts' did not embrace local fairs and carnivals, circus, variety, musicals, folk singing, ballroom dancing, dressmaking, evensong, landscape gardening, films and the cinema, family weddings, amateur dramatics, local choirs or radio – a (rather odd) list which might well stand as illustration of a quintessentially British culture (Eliot, 1948).

The lessons to be drawn from this brief account are clear enough for those working in Britain, but they have a wider application. Both in democracies and in totalitarian regimes, the arts administrator has a duty, so far as is possible, to redress wrong judgement, and to counter the imbalances which may have led us unfairly to denigrate a particular kind of art, art form, unfavoured artist, or art of a neglected region.

Over the decades there are many things which can distort true judgement: political and economic upheaval, industrial revolution, colonial imperialisms and class warfare can, for example, render the state's valuation of art unbalanced and wrong. Yet the arts administrator must constantly be looking for opportunities to redress the balance, for in no country is the artistic canon permanently fixed. Though the arts bureaucrat is often the servant of the state, and must accept the state's view of the cultural map, by contrast the arts administrator must never allow the parameters of art to become fixed in his mind simply by official custom and habit. The good arts administrator will always retain a lively sense of critical revaluation.

REFERENCES

Amis, K. (1989) *'Setting the arts free'*, in Butler, E. *et al.*, *The Art of the State* (1989).
Arts Council of Great Britain (1985/6) *Annual Report*.
Bacon, Rev. M.J. (1894) *Diaries*.
Bancroft, S. and Bancroft, M. (1888) *Mr and Mrs Bancroft On and Off the Stage*.
Eliot, T.S. (1948) *Notes Towards the Definition of Culture*.

Hall, S. (1984) 'The Culture Gap', in *Marxism Today* (January, 1984).

Harker, J. (undated) 'Journal', in *A Victorian Poacher*, Christian, G. (ed.) (1979).

Harrison, J.F.C. (1984) *The Common People*.

Hewison, R. (1981) *Under Siege: Literary Life in London 1939–1945*.

Irving, H. (1883) *The Drama Addresses*.

Keynes, Maynard (1945) 'The Arts Council: its policy and hopes', in *The Listener* (12 July, 1945).

Kilvert, Rev. F. (1987) *Kilvert's Diary 1870–1879*.

Malcolmson, R. (1973) *Popular Recreations in English Society 1700–1850*.

Pick, J. and Anderton, M. (1990) *Industrial Support for the Arts*.

Thompson, E.P. (1980) *The Making of the English Working Class*.

Williams, R. (1960) 'The Magic System', in *Problems in Materialism and Culture* (1980).

Williams, R. (1976) *Keywords*.

2.1 ADMINISTRATION AND ORGANIZATIONS

The arts do not consist of the sum total of arts organizations within a country, any more than they may be fully described by an account of a 'cultural economy'. Nevertheless, arts administrators must work for, and with (even sometimes against) organizations of all kinds. It is essential therefore that the administrator has a keen sense of the way organizations may be classified, from whence they derive their power and authority, and how they work internally and with each other.

The arts administrator is most likely to work for discrete arts organizations. In general these are either created to promote a particular art form, group of artists, or artist, or to run venues, travelling shows or festivals. Such arts organizations may be private or public companies, or (characteristically) a mixture of the two: non-profit-distributing limited companies with charitable aims and status. There is now, in Britain, a greater mix of commercial and charitable organizations within the arts sector.

He or she is, next, most likely to work for an arts department of a larger organization, such as the arts and recreation department of a local government authority, or the arts department of a body with wider purposes, such as the British Council. After that, the arts administrator is most likely to work with an arts regulatory and funding body (such as an Arts Ministry) or an advocacy and research body (such as a Tourist Authority). A growing number of former and part-time arts administrators also work for private consultancies, usually small two- or three-person units which work alongside larger organizations.

Finally, the arts administrator is likely to work with (and sometimes against) a wide range of other public and private bodies which, though they are not set up for the purposes of promulgating the arts, nevertheless set the general legal, fiscal and educational parameters within which art is presented and which mould the audience for them. Almost all kinds of organization can at some time be brought into this category, but such public organizations would normally include in particular national and local government, the courts and other parts of the legal system, the schools and education system, charities, trusts and the tax authorities. Private organizations in this category include manufacturing and service industry, supporters clubs and all kinds of societies ranging from sports clubs to special interest groups.

Etzioni (1961) first developed what has become a standard model for understanding the internal mechanisms of organizations and the way they work together. He first suggested that there were three kinds of power which those in authority may use to control those in lower positions within the organization:

- **Coercive power**, which depends upon threat of punishment or reprisal.
- **Remunerative power**, which depends upon material rewards such as money or increased leisure time.
- **Normative power**, which depends upon the allocation of symbolic rewards of esteem and prestige.

Etzioni argues that although organizations tend to employ all three kinds of power, different kinds of organization tend to emphasize only one. He then goes on to set out three broad ways in which those in lower positions react to the way authority is primarily exercised in their organization. This Etzioni calls their cathetic-evaluative 'orientation', or more simply their *involvement*:

- **Alienative involvement** is strong disapproval, hostility and compliance only under threat.
- **Calculative involvement** is relative indifference, depending upon the rewards obtained through commitment.
- **Moral involvement** is strong approval of the authorities, based on a shared commitment to the organization's values and aims.

With these categories in mind he is able to construct a table, in which the different kinds of power which may be exercised within an organization are set against the orientation or involvement of those working within it (Table 2.1):

Table 2.1 Kinds of power and involvement

Kinds of power	*Kinds of involvement*		
	Alienative	Calculative	Moral
Coercive	1 (Coercive)	2	3
Remunerative	4	5 (Utilitarian)	6
Normative	7	8	9 (Normative)

It will be seen that in theory there are nine types of relationships between authority and those in lower positions. Etzioni argues that three in particular are more effective, because the kind of authority exercised is matched by the type of involvement sought by the rest of the organization. These three congruent relationships Etzioni respectively terms the **coercive** organization, the **utilitarian** organization and the **normative** organization.

Before proceeding further, it is useful to begin to apply Etzioni's model to the situation in which the arts administrator works. Most arts organizations will be normative organizations. The work-force will broadly share the organization's values and aims, and, like the administrator, will work more for moral than for calculative reasons. The administrator's authority will be exercised in a normative way. (Experience suggests that arts workers do not usually 'take instructions'; they are more likely to complain of being in 'one long round of meetings' which never seem to come to final decisions.)

However, many of the other bodies with which the arts organization has to deal will be utilitarian, or even coercive in nature. When one of these brings pressure to bear upon the normative organization – if, for example, a utilitarian funding body makes its further support dependent upon a radical change in the arts organization's programme – then the administrator is placed in a dilemma, for organizational power must now be exercised in two conflicting ways. The administrator must either try to deal with the outside body in the usual normative way, involving the outsiders in open discussions with the arts organization's workforce, or must try to railroad the funding body's wishes through the internal consultation systems, which may well upset colleagues used to working in a more democratic way. The modern arts administrator is frequently confronted by this kind of dilemma. (State bodies frequently exert pressure upon arts organizations to change their organizational structure, so that they too are essentially utilitarian, and can more easily mesh with the state's bureaucratic structures.)

Etzioni elaborates further, and in the process suggests the reason why arts organizations work best when they have normative characteristics. He divides general organizational aims, or goals, into three general categories:

- **Order goals** cover organizations which exist to control deviant behaviour.
- **Economic goals** belong to those producing goods and service.
- **Cultural goals** are set by organizations creating and preserving symbolic objects.

And, taking his earlier description of the three 'stable' kinds of organizational relationship, he creates a second model (Table 2.2):

Table 2.2 Kinds of organization

Types of organization (Compliance structures)	Organizational goals		
	Order	Economic	Cultural
Coercive	1	2	3
Utilitarian	4	5	6
Normative	7	8	9

Again, it is clear that there are nine possible relationships between the goals of an organization and its internal structures. But, as before, three of them (1, 5 and 9) are said to be particularly stable.

If Etzioni's hypothesis is accepted, then it follows that an arts organization (which has cultural goals) will be most stable when its internal organizational characteristics are normative in character. Equally, it would follow that a state funding agency, which has economic goals, will stabilize around a utilitarian form. It is a final part of Etzioni's thesis that organizations from different categories do not find it easy to work together, which explains some (though not all) of the conflicts in the arts world between administration and bureaucracy, often between arts organizations and the funding bodies with whom they must work. Their organizational natures are fundamentally at odds.

However we analyse its causes, the conflict is a familiar one to the arts administrator. Certainly it is helpful to understand its nature. The effects can nevertheless be minimized by following two important guidelines. First, it is essential that within an 'open', normative arts organization, there is a detailed internal dissemination of information about all negotiations with outside bodies which the administrator and colleagues undertake. If that is done, then the staff will be able to support the administrator realistically in any confrontation. If it is not, conflict will surprise them, and they will feel that their previous identification with the values and aims of the organization has been undervalued by their boss.

Second, all organizations have to be able to take decisions, and to act upon them. Alongside the ongoing dissemination of information, the administrator must have in place clear systems both for taking decisions and for ensuring they are carried out. It must be clear in meetings what is being discussed, what are the alternative conclusions that may be reached, and how an agreed decision is to be arrived at. When (hopefully) that decision is made, it must be clear who is carrying it forward, by which means, and when he or she is to report on the outcome.

It is already clear that the administrator has to play many different roles. The arts administrator is critic, planner, communicator, catalyst, energizer, negotiator and enabler all at once. In a normative organization these many tasks require constant and informed support, which in turn requires the administrator to be in continuous dialogue with colleagues. It is therefore important to look briefly at the nature of the administrator's own authority within the arts organization.

The classic definition of the nature of authority (Weber, 1947) will be helpful here:

There are three pure types of legitimate authority. The validity of their claims to legitimacy may be based on:

1. **Rational Grounds** – resting on a belief in the 'legality' of patterns of normative rules, and the right of those elevated to authority under such rules to issue commands (legal authority).

2. **Traditional Grounds** – resting on an established belief in the sanctity of immemorial traditions and the legitimacy of the status of those exercising authority under them (traditional authority).

3. **Charismatic Grounds** – resting on devotion to the specific and exceptional sanctity, heroism and exemplary character of an individual person (charismatic authority).

Arts administrators may assume their authority in any of these three ways. Someone running a theatre for a local government may well be tightly enmeshed in legal and procedural red tape, and gain their authority simply by occupying the post and following detailed rules. (For such a person charisma may be a positive disadvantage.) The director of a well-established music festival may conversely have few written rules as guidance, but may gain authority simply by occupying a post with a long and significant history. And there once were many 'heroic' arts administrators who are forever linked with organizations which they began, or which they led through their finest hours, whose charisma seemed to light up the organization and whose administrative practices will still be remembered (and followed) long after their departure.

Administrators who work either on traditional authority or charismatic authority will have one important problem in common. Their authority is given to them in part by such things as the status of the job ('The new director of the Uptown Festival!') or their forceful personality ('Mr Hecks dominates press conferences and is a wonderful speaker on television!') but it is also an authority continuously ceded to them by those with whom they work. If colleagues become seriously dissatisfied, then they can withdraw their support ('Ms Why is not up to the job', or 'Zedd's time is past') and neither the traditions of the post, nor their charisma will be likely to save them.

Such administrators need therefore to be in constant dialogue with all of those with whom they work: goal-setting, praising, censuring and planning together. They will follow many of the practices of team management (Chapter 9 below). At best, colleagues will feel that the way the organization moves is determined in partnership, and that it is not therefore a matter solely for a distant 'heroic' leader. Successful charismatic leaders have an ability to create a communal team sense of identity and purpose. Junior members of the organization will say of its leaders that they 'always had time for a word with me'. An example would be the BBC when, according to Burns' analysis, it was successfully led (Burns, 1964).

In a more bureaucratic organization, when the administrator exercises legal authority, contact will tend, as Weber (1947, op. cit.) pointed out, to be impersonal, and all decisions and instructions will refer to an agreed and detailed set of rules. Constant consultation and internal dialogue are not needed in such organizations.

There are other differences too. In the first two cases – which include a large number, perhaps a majority, of arts organizations – working contact between staff tends to continue outside working hours and outside the working spaces. The home tends, for such administrators, to be an extension of the office. They tend to be 'on call' continuously, and to take few holidays. In the more bureaucratic organization, such as a local government office, after-work contact between staff tends to be restricted to communal recreation interests or clearly designated 'social' meetings.

These constructs may be a way of explaining the administrative tension which sometimes exists between arts organizations and their paymasters and/or controllers. In government and neo-government departments decisions are made according to clearly laid down procedures, and without the charged and general dialogue that often accompanies decision-taking in an arts organization. Their method of communication is formal: bureaucrats write rather than talk. Moreover, arts organizations are not infrequently at their liveliest at the very times which are 'after hours' for bureaucrats. (Everyone recalls cases where local authorities refused to sign cheques after 5 p.m. for artists coming to play one-night stands in their civic theatres!) In all, creating effective communications between bureaucratic organizations and arts organizations is fraught with difficulty.

Such considerations make it imperative that the arts administrator is well aware of which kind of authority they can best wield. If the organization they administer does not suit their administrative style there is a mutually damaging mismatch, and both sides suffer. We now turn to the subject of work orientation in more detail.

2.2 WORK ORIENTATION

The notion of work orientation was first developed by Goldthorpe (1966) who defined it as 'an ordering of wants and expectations relative to work'. Key concepts are that work orientation can be fully understood only when seen in the context of what people were looking for when they first entered that work, and of the changing expectations in their lives outside the workplace.

Goldthorpe *et al.* (1968) identified three initial work orientations. When someone chooses a job because of the high pay it offers, this can be called **'instrumental orientation'**. When job entrants are influenced by the good prospects of promotion within their organization, this is **'bureaucratic orientation'**, or when it is primarily the prospect of camaraderie with their fellow workers which attracts them this can be called **'solidaristic orientation'**. These are **prior orientations** (the expectations when people enter work). Equally important however are what Watson (1980) calls **dynamic orientations**, the ever-shifting wants and expectancies, once in the job, caused by changes in home, work and leisure circumstances.

All this builds upon the models we discussed above, but it is still insufficiently sophisticated to take account of the highly complex orientation of arts administrators (and arts bureaucrats). Accordingly, Anderton (1987), in his researches into the work orientation of cinema managers, followed by work in other arts organizations, added three further categories of orientation to the standard models, making a total of six:

1. instrumental orientation
2. career orientation (bureaucratic)
3. unitary orientation (solidaristic)
4. product orientation
5. entrepreneurial orientation
6. practice orientation.

These six pure or ideal types are analytical constructs which may help the arts administrator question why he or she is engaged in the occupation, and may also be a useful aid for assessing the appropriateness of applicants for working in a particular arts administration environment.

1. The instrumentally-oriented arts administrator

This type, which Etzioni (1961) called 'calculative', is easy to define as an ideal, but extremely difficult to discover in the flesh. None of those interviewed in Anderton's research claimed to be working solely for the salary. Indeed the vast majority claimed to be working in the arts despite the salary. Occasionally, however, an underlying instrumental orientation could be detected. One cinema manager interviewed by Anderton claimed at an early interview: 'I am the ambassador for my company ... and I try to instil the same attitude in my staff.' Nine months later, when told that his retirement date would not be extended by the company, he said: 'I am working strictly to rule from now on. No overtime. Nothing. The company has made it clear it does not want me, so....'

In some cases (particularly in precariously-funded small organizations) it was clear that administrators felt that an instrumental orientation to their work would be in vain, as there was no more money available to reward extra effort. In cinemas, and resort venues, where bonus systems operated, there was some evidence of increased instrumental orientation. There, managers and administrators claimed to have little or no time for leisure pursuits principally because they worked long hours to meet bonus targets.

2. The career-oriented arts administrator

The research encountered some examples of career-oriented arts administrators, although many branches of arts administration do not offer a career structure stable enough for aspirants simply to work their way up one organizational ladder. Usually they were what William Watson (1964) termed 'spiralists': career-oriented people who move frequently between organizations to gain advancement. Such people make great efforts in their early years to make themselves worthy of promotion: working unsocial hours, looking for opportunities to promote the well-being of the organization they are working for, forgoing social life, and being careful not to become conspicuously attached to unfashionable or minority causes.

It is noteworthy that there are few generalist arts administrators (though many generalist arts bureaucrats). The research encountered theatre managers who had formerly been actors, and cinema managers who had once been usherettes, but little evidence that music administrators could (or would wish to) move over to run galleries, or that cinema managers could run orchestras. This points to a further distinction between arts bureaucrats (who are frequently generalists or working in art forms of which they do not have extensive knowledge or experience) and arts administrators, who almost always have had lengthy acquaintanceship with the art form they are working in.

3. The unitary-oriented arts administrator

The unitary approach identifies itself primarily with the organization's staff, or even with the organization itself, when work-force and enterprise are seen as one, as with a proselytizing theatre company, or gay art group. Sometimes the unitary response is latent, only becoming evident when, for example, someone is unjustly sacked. In the course of Anderton's research a private cinema owner decided to close his cinema and sell the site for development. Manager and staff closed ranks, and published and then distributed leaflets opposing the scheme. They also canvassed local politicians to such an extent that the owner partly relented and a satisfactory compromise was reached. When the site was redeveloped it included a new cinema.

The rapid turnover of staff in arts organizations is often thought to be a good thing; for some years the Arts Council of Great Britain had an 'unwritten rule' that more than five years in an arts job was 'too long'. This, combined with the high rate of mortality amongst smaller arts organizations, means that, although arts administrators frequently claim that they would like to be wholly committed to one unit for a considerable time, in practice it is rarely possible to be so.

4. The product-oriented arts administrator

This is the person who is so consumately interested in one art form, or even in one branch of it, that they will identify it as their main leisure interest. Such a person may not, of course, be actively engaged in working in their favoured art, and this 'product orientation' may cause them to be less interested in their working than in their leisure time. Research in this area has highlighted another possible difficulty, when a 'number two' is strongly interested in the art with which his or her organization deals, but resents the fact that the boss makes the decisions and meets most of the interesting people.

There are, of course, many enthusiasts who are fine administrators, but it is important to emphasize that enthusiasm without critical discrimination, administrative knowledge and political skill is useless. Nevertheless, many enthusiasts in this study, who were plainly product-oriented but equally plainly knowledgeable administrators, demonstrated that this is a highly desirable additional quality to have; people spoke of their enthusiasm as 'infectious'.

5. The entrepreneurially-oriented administrator

This type, usually an arts bureaucrat rather than an arts administrator, seeks constantly to broaden the scope of the organization, placing it sometimes within the wider context of showbusiness, with the accent on 'business', and sometimes in a wider context still. Research examples included both art gallery and museum curators who introduced lunch hour recitals, theatre managers who included film series, and early music groups that included period dancing. Organizations shaped by entrepreneurially-oriented people tend to have three characteristics: i) there is no 'moral' concern about the programme, or about items on sale, greater than their sales potential; ii) the aims of the organization can readily become diffuse, if that retains commercial viability; and iii) the administrator does not have an overriding commitment to the organization, and is usually happy to 'moonlight', or make deals for his or her own benefit with 'rival' organizations.

6. The practice-oriented arts administrator

In a surprising number of cases the research suggested that it was the job itself which was the main attraction. Interviewees repeatedly said that they liked the totality of the work: the people, the air of commitment, the paper work and even the ambience of arts buildings. The disadvantages of the job: low salary, long and unsocial hours, insecure future, variable product and intense (even overwhelming) competition from other leisure industries seemed, paradoxically, to be further attractions rather than disadvantages. This gives credence to the claims made by Peters and Waterman (1982) that we 'desperately need meaning in our lives and will sacrifice a great deal to institutions that will provide meaning for us'.

Love of the job for its own sake did sometimes lead to workaholism, but many interviewees cited the fact that they could arrange their working hours, or days off, to suit their domestic arrangements and this was a great source of satisfaction to them. One arts manager said that although she could earn almost twice as much if she returned to teaching, she found the freedom of being able to arrange her own hours and intensity of work was sufficient compensation. On a separate point, Daniel (1973) suggested that the job itself, when of central interest, produces a concern for the quality of the work undertaken and for the social contacts that can occur (although dedication to the job is in itself no guarantee of good results). On the whole, practice-oriented arts administrators seemed to work considerably extended hours, and there was, sadly, some evidence that their domestic relationships tended to suffer as a result.

The nature of the organization, and orientation to his or her work within it, do not of course fully explain an arts administrator's behaviour. As we shall elaborate in the following chapter, arts organizations, and their administrators, vary widely in size, scope and nature. Moreover the nature of an organization varies from week to week according to the pressures placed upon it by the organizations and groups upon which it is reliant for various resources. Such pressure groupings are sometimes called **constituencies**.

The arts administrator's organization is almost always part of an environment that includes constituencies upon which it is reliant for resources, such as employees, artists and their agents, sponsors, journalists, printers, inspectors and customers. Many of them demand resources in return, and the administrator has constantly to balance and assess the priority, at any given time, of the demands of each constituency. Miles (1980) suggested that, ideally, 'organizational effectiveness' could be achieved by satisfying such demands in a manner that minimalizes dependence on them, but continues their support at a level which will ensure long-term effectiveness.

The arts administrator is unusually dependent upon external resources and, unlike those in manufacturing industries, supply of them is often highly dependent upon political whim and the vagaries of current taste. We have already noted the increased enmeshing of the funding bodies with the administration of arts organizations, and have also noted the increasingly complex bureaucracies that are such a crucial external resource for the modern administrator (or administrative team). This can be more clearly demonstrated if we divide the constituencies with whom the administrator must deal into three: overseer, internal and external.

- **Overseer constituencies** This category includes all those upon whom the administration is wholly dependent, and whose withdrawal of support could, at any time, result in the collapse of the organization. It includes all the funding and licensing bodies with whom the organization deals, together with the owners of all buildings, transport and equipment that are leased or rented. 'Mixed funding' and the 'matching grants' systems create an ever more complex range of overseer constituencies for grant-aided arts organizations. The need for 'strategies' and for continuous 'assessment' imposes greater administrative strains upon the organization, and gives the funding bodies a greater degree of control in shaping their functions. The greater number of overseer constituencies which non-facility-based arts and entertainment groups have, and their comparative lack of stabilizing internal constituencies also means that they are at higher risk of collapse.
- **Internal constituencies** These include all full- and part-time, paid and voluntary staff who play a part in the running of the organization. Internal resources usually act as a counterbalance to external pressures. Modern systems of arts funding, however, involve an increasing number of internal

constituencies with a second function, that of assessing and auditing the organization from within. Consultants, for example, will often seem to be acting as an internal constituency but, on the other hand, they will also be seen by external or overseer constituencies as a part of their resources. Modern systems thus tend towards the break-up of organizational autonomy, and make the kind of holistic management we advocate much harder to achieve – but, paradoxically, even more necessary.

- **External constituencies** In this category are those resources of which the organization has essential need, but between which it can make choices. External constituencies thus range from the artists and shows from which the programmer chooses, to the more basic suppliers of office equipment, food and drink, cleaning services and programmes. Perhaps the most important external constituency is the audience, not merely for economic reasons, but, as we have already argued, because a response from an audience is a condition of art existing at all.

It is fatally easy to become so concerned with pressures from the overseer constituencies that the external constituencies are overlooked. Pleasing the sponsor can become so important that pleasing the public becomes secondary. One of the most embarrassing sights in recent years was the televised opening of the Birmingham Symphony Hall in 1992. Everything seemed set for total success. The administration was a first-rate team; the funding bodies, the EEC officials and the Birmingham City Corporation, had worked together splendidly and were well satisfied. The Arts Council-funded City of Birmingham Symphony Orchestra was at the height of its powers. Yet, the cameras roamed over rows of empty seats. In accommodating the wishes of the overseer funding bodies, the need to assemble an audience had apparently been forgotten.

It becomes ever harder, if not impossible, to 'minimalize' overseer resource dependency. The difficulty is so great that some arts administrators feel they have lost the independence to present the kind of programme they would like in ways they think right to the people they think proper. Like the cinema manager who was made to retire at a time of his overseers' choosing, they tend to 'work to rule', as bureaucrats within a resented system, rather than as the practice-oriented administrators they once were.

REFERENCES

Anderton, M. (1987) *Cinema Management.*
Burns, T. (1964) *Commitment and Career in the BBC.*
Daniel, M.W. (1973) 'Understanding employee behaviour in its context' in *Man and Organization*, ed. Child, J. (1973).
Etzioni, A. (1961) *Comparative Analysis of Complex Organizations.*
Goldthorpe, J.H. (1966) 'Attitudes and behaviour of car assembly workers' in *British Journal of Sociology*, 17(3) (Sept., 1966).
Goldthorpe, J.H. *et al.* (1968) *The Affluent Worker: Industrial Attitudes and Behaviour.*
Miles, R.H. (1980) *Macro Organizational Behaviour.*

Peters, T.J. and Waterman, R.H. Jnr (1982) *In Search of Excellence.*

Watson, T.J. (1980) *Sociology, Work and Industry.*

Watson, W. (1964) 'Social mobility and social class in industrial communities' in *Closed Systems and Open Minds*, ed. Gluckmann, M. and Devon, E. (1964).

Weber, M. (1947) *The Theory of Social and Economic Organisation.*

Development of arts administration systems

3

3.1 FORMS OF ARTS ADMINISTRATION

In each country the different realms of the arts are simultaneously administered in a variety of quite different ways. Some of these are traditional, others derive from clear historical causes, others are effectively imposed by government legislation. Some ways of administering the arts are subject to constant change as legal frameworks change. Others remain unaltered through changes of government, revolution, or war. For example, the Bolshoi continued to be administered in much the same way after the Russian revolution as before it, in French country fairs they still 'bottle' the crowds in the nineteenth century way, and in some form or other in most advanced countries the bucolic arts continue to be administered (and to flourish) in much the same way that they have always done alongside sophisticated theme parks and the apparently pervasive media.

It is useful to separate five main segments in the development of modern arts administration:

- the bucolic
- the commercial
- the 'mixed service'
- the planned
- the mega-corporate.

In Britain it is possible to say that these different ways of administering the arts can, broadly, be placed in a developing historical sequence, but that is not necessarily so elsewhere. A country with a more dominant religious tradition is likely to have 'the planned' predominant. A country which has achieved independence after colonial rule is likely to have to plan to revive the bucolic. Some socialist countries have ideological objections to the mega-corporate.

Nor are the five groups by any means separate entities. A good deal of arts administration involves elements of two or more of these. Moreover, each can readily be subdivided. For our purposes, however, the following five models give us a useful analytical tool.

The bucolic

Bucolic arts administration is usually undertaken by unpaid workers, who feel it incumbent upon them to maintain a cultural tradition in their locality. The planning of village fêtes, carnivals and fairs, Shrove Tuesday galas, carol singing, harvest suppers, choir concerts, Easter parades, community pantomimes, dances, local artists' shows, flower festivals, storytelling evenings, church organ recitals and well dressing might be the kinds of activities that in Britain we term 'bucolic'. This local culture thrives in Britain. An interesting series of publications from the Women's Institutes, describing life in the villages of each British County (1989 ff.) gave, for example, an astonishingly rich and varied picture of the small cultural events which enrich the lives of so many people in Britain, and which are rarely included in any survey of 'the arts'.

Such activities are set up for a local audience, often annually, sometimes seasonally, and administered according to local custom rather than by a rule-book. They are usually run by loosely-constituted committees rather than one designated administrator, and usually run in a 'normative' way (pp. 28–29). However, the administrative group will sometimes be 'fronted' by a figurehead. The late Arthur Marshall (1990), who was President of his Devon village's annual show, gave us an affectionate insight into the ways of village administration:

> I had been honoured by being made this year's President of the Appleton and District Horticultural Society Show. Never mind, for it was a splendid affair altogether, which several lively meetings in the village hall had preceded. One of the economically advantageous items at a Show is the Draw Tickets (for various prizes). At one of our meetings, the dear lady, no longer in the first flush of youth, who has been running, with willing volunteers, the selling of Draw Tickets for the last twenty years, attempted very tentatively to withdraw from her task. No hope at all and she was gently and politely shunted back into it, a despairing smile on her face showing everybody that she had had, from the first, no hope whatever in succeeding in her bid for freedom. In most villages, and when somebody takes on a job, it is assumed ('the floral arrangements are, as ever, in the capable hands of Mrs Bowsher') that they will continue with it until they drop.

Further apparently casual administrative arrangements can be found still in the amateur group administration of the popular arts. In Britain, hostility by official-dom towards the professional circus has, rather oddly, been accompanied by a significant growth of interest in circus skills, particularly in juggling. This is underpinned by a strong commercial interest – most large cities now have two or three specialist shops selling juggling equipment – but is essentially a grassroots amateur movement, sometimes supported by funding organizations but carried forward by loosely organized amateur groups. Such juggling groups have regular meetings and teaching networks, arrange public shows (often for charity) and have huge conventions. Yet all is arranged *ad hoc*, by general discussion and popular assent, and as a result the publicity material (Figure 2) with its casual vernacular, low prices, and laid-back style resembles a much earlier decade.

7th British Juggling Convention
Manchester
14th - 17th April 1994
Hopwood Hall

About the Site

Hopwood Hall is seven miles north of Manchester and is situated in 70 acres of countryside and woods, just 2 miles from the M62 and close to Rail Links (B.R. Castleton is 10 minutes away by bus.) There are 2 sports halls, a dance studio space for workshops, room for masses of traders, great accommodation- 300 beds on site , camping / van park.], Good, cheap food - veggie, vegan and omnivore will be provided by Hopwood Hall and there are excellent creche / kids facilities and even a fitness centre (for a small charge)

About the Convention

All the favourites will be there , the renegade stage, workshops on every conceivable subject and of course the Public Show . The Grand Parade and games will take place in Manchester City Centre - transport will be laid-on . Skylight Circus will be opening their aerial facilities in Rochdale , (10 minutes from Hopwood) for the entire weekend . Places will be limited so let us know in advance

How you can help

Most of all by getting your registration form and dosh to us A.S.A.P.-There has been no AJC final this year, so we are running on air at the moment .Plus volunteers are always needed !So please indicate on the form if you can help with; stewarding, workshopping or performing.

Further information

If you have any problems, questions, answers, useful tips etc, then there is a 24 hour convention hotline!! 061 - 834 8483 (At the moment it's part human, part ansa-phone, but will become more human as the convention gets nearer!)

This Convention is Organised by Manchester Jugglers and North West Circus Network .We acknowledge the help and support of the BJF, City of Drama ,Central Manchester Development Corporation and N.W.A.B.

I would like to pre-register for the following days
(please fill in number of people per day, and include all names and addresses on a separate sheet of paper)

Adults all days			@£18.00 =	
Under 16's all days			@ £9.00 =	
Friday		Adults	@ £8.00 =	
		Under 16's	@ £4.00 =	
Saturday		Adults	@£10.00 =	
		Under 16's	@ £5.00 =	
Sunday		Adults	@ £5.00 =	
		Under 16's	@ £2.50 =	

Type of accommodation, room / van / camping (delete as necessary)
There are twin-bed rooms available at £9.00 per person
I require ....rooms for..........people for..........nights

I enclose a cheque for the total amount of   £..................
made payable to:- ANNUAL JUGGLING CONVENTION LTD.

Creche required for (number)..........children aged..........

I will require ....car permits.   I want to use the Aerial Facility ☐
I can offer help in (tick)   ☐ Stewarding
                                        ☐ Performing/Workshops (inc. details)
Name..
Address..
....Post Code..........

Telephone ....
Please return this form to: Annual Juggling Convention Ltd.
                                              % 27 Ashwood Avenue,
                                              West Didsbury,
                                              Manchester,
                                              M20 8TB

Figure 2 7th British Juggling Convention

Amateur administration does not of course mean that performers are necessarily amateur. There are more than 300 professional agencies in Britain supplying 'acts' (falconry, high wire, motor bike stunts, clowns, dramatized battles complete with cannon and charging horses, marching bands, jousting, fire-eating, trapeze acts, large-scale illusions, to amateur-run 'shows' and galas, private parties and street festivals, at fees ranging from £50 to £15 000.

But it is the scale of amateur involvement which is more impressive. An extensive 1991 survey found that 53% of all adults in Britain claimed to take an active part in some form of arts or crafts. The fifteen most popular activities are listed here by percentage:

	%
Photography	19
Disco dancing	11
Textile crafts	11
Woodwork	10
Painting and drawing	8
Playing musical instrument (solo)	5
Other crafts	5
Metalwork	4
Ballroom dancing	4
Writing stories	4
Making videos	4
Drama	2
Writing poetry	2
Choir	2
Pop music	2

A glance in any local newspaper or parish magazine will show evidence of a vast network of amateur societies: some directly educational in nature, others formed to bring together people with similar interests, others as 'friends' linked to a professional arts centre. There are networks of poetry-lovers, fan clubs of famous performers, art societies, photographic societies, watercolorists, tap dancing groups, history and archaeological groups, writers' guilds, amateur choirs and orchestras, barber-shop harmony groups, morris dancers, amateur film clubs, and many others. An important underlying point is the revived importance of entertainment in the home. A 1985 survey for example showed that 76% of Londoners regularly watched television with their families, 55% read books at home one or more times a week and 69% regularly 'entertained' at home, as against 57% in 1981.

More formal are the music societies, amateur dramatic societies and amateur operatic societies that thrive in almost every town and city in Britain. They meet many of the conditions of 'bucolic' art; they are amateur-run, local in their appeal and interest, performing to a fixed and 'traditional' calendar. They are predominantly urban, rather than rural, and date only from the nineteenth century, and so are not embedded in traditional culture like the much older rural activities mentioned above.

Nevertheless the scale of the involvement in such amateur activities is impressive. The National Federation of Music Societies, the national body for such amateur groups, has pointed out that the NFMS is the largest single concert promoter in the UK. Amateur organizations currently spend £5.7m annually on professional fees, promoting 6060 concerts to more than 1 360 000 people. Figures for amateur drama are equally impressive. There are in Britain some 8500 amateur societies, and on any evening there are likely to be in excess of 550 amateur drama performances in Britain (against some 200 professional ones). As the average attendance at an amateur performance is calculated to be just under 150, there are more than 24 million attendances each year at amateur drama performances in Britain – as against the 6 million attendances at subsidized professional performances.

In the world of large-scale amateur opera production, administrative problems approach the scale of small professional productions. Amateur operatic societies have many of the same production costs as a professional company (though scenery and costumes are usually hired, which is cheaper and easier than having them designed), and, because the director, musical director and orchestra are not infrequently paid, larger societies have some of the same administrative problems over employer's liabilities. In general, they use a local professional venue – sometimes nowadays as a co-production with the professional theatre administration – so they have similar marketing, booking, licensing and house management responsibilities to a professional management.

Murdin (1993) reported that one such group, the Leeds Thespians Amateur Operatic Society, tried to present their 1993 show in the usual way. They found that even with a rebate on the normal booking rate for the Leeds Grand (£13 500 a week) the costs for their production of *Gentlemen Prefer Blondes* exceeded £40 000. (The 14-piece orchestra, which had to be paid Musicians Union rates, alone cost £4000.) Despite intensive publicity, the show played to only 35% capacity and lost £10 000. On the other hand, in the same year, a co-production of *Annie* at the Hull New Theatre, produced jointly by the amateur Northern Theatre Company and the New Theatre's professional management, made a small profit. So at this end of the amateur spectrum, the risk now taken by amateur administrations is formidable, and what may at one time have been a pleasant local hobby is now being drawn inevitably into the realms of commercial administration.

The commercial

Through the eighteenth and early nineteenth century in Britain the bucolic arts existed side by side with the commercial world of the travelling showmen. By 'commercial' we here mean those professionally administered shows, exhibitions and publications where the art is a market commodity, and where success, and indeed existence, is wholly dependent upon selling the commodities in the open market.

For a brief period in the second half of the eighteenth century the professional British arts, from the foremost poets and painters of the day to the scruffiest travelling showmen, were almost wholly commercial. Poets, musicians and painters readily supported themselves on the open market. Alexander Pope made £4000 from *The Iliad* alone; in their different musical realms J.C. Bach, Arne and Haydn all became rich men; Hogarth made a fortune from his prints; and when the painter Reynolds died he left £175 000. The music shop, print shop and book shop took their places in the High Street alongside the butcher and the baker, and the newspapers intermingled advertisements for kitchenware and clothing with those of portrait painters, musicians and dancing masters.

The arts were enjoyed in large cosmopolitan venues, such as the great pleasure gardens of Vauxhall and Ranelagh, which presented concerts to a much wider audience than went to subscription concerts. The varied entertainment at Vauxhall was memorably described in *Vanity Fair* (1847–48):

> The fiddlers in cocked hats, who played ravishing melodies under the gilded cockleshell in the midst of the Gardens; the singers, both of comic and sentimental ballads; the country dances, formed by bouncing cockneys and cockneyesses ... the signal which announced that Madame Saqui was about to mount skyward on a slack rope ... while Mrs Salmon performed the Battle of Borodino (a savage cantata against the Corsican upstart).

Of equal importance were the coffee houses which proliferated in the larger towns and cities – Trevelyan (1959) calculates there were more than 500 in London alone – commercial enterprises which also offered exhibitions, music, libraries, discussion and daily newspapers for their clientele, in effect, the ambience of a modern arts club without the restraints of closed membership.

Meanwhile some 8000 showmen travelled the byways of Britain, going the long-established rounds of the traditional country fairs with sideshows as various as those later described by Thomas Hardy (1886): '... persons whose activities found a congenial field among the peep-shows, toy-stands, waxworks, inspired monsters, disinterested medical men who travelled for the public good, thimble-riggers, nick-nack vendors, and readers of Fate.' But as the dawning industrial revolution began to draw rural dwellers into the new towns things became more difficult for the travelling showmen, as Richard Barnard (1913), a marionette proprietor, graphically recalls in his memoirs:

> When we arrived in London, we were at a loss to know where to go, or what to do. We went South and got a room in St. Mary's Square. After collecting my few props, which I had left behind, I found the children had been having a performance in the garden with them, whenever they felt inclined and I was compelled to replace them. I was very busy getting the few things together and in order, and secured an engagement at the Criterion Music Hall, Sheerness. One week for £5.0.0d. At least I think this was the salary. I engaged an old hand, at Marionette working (and who was also a dulcimer player) to assist us. We worked the week, and after paying fares, etc. 25/- salary and lodgings, I had not much left. We had nothing to do or either anything in view, for the following weeks. The proprietor a Mr. Kennedy made me an offer to remain on share terms, to work the week, and take a benefit on the Friday night, but with his prices being so low, and Hall very small, when the Proprietor took his expenses from the takings my share would be about 30/-. A school performance I

gave on Saturday raised 11/-. This amount just paid the man and his lodgings. I next took an offer of a room at a public house at Milton, my Father's native place. I tried my luck by giving some performances but it was a failure, the takings not being enough to pay the rent, and had it not been for the kindness of the landlady and her husband who refused the rent we should have had to go without food. I did not know now what to try. The man I had with me become ill so had to pay his fare to London.

Towards the end of the nineteenth century, the travelling showpeople with their travelling booths, were increasingly swallowed into larger organizations. Larger units of travelling showpeople – Richardsons, Wombwells and Sangers – bought up the smaller fry for their much larger menageries and circuses. Elsewhere, showbusiness began to be dominated by large oligarchies of management, while the artists began also to organize themselves into power blocks. The individual music hall proprietors banded together in their own management association, to be met by the music hall performers' massed strike of 1907. The end of the nineteenth century saw the birth of the Theatrical Managers' Association and the growth of the vast national variety circuits of Stoll and Moss (Pick, 1983; 1985).

Almost the last bastion of the small commercial entrepreneur in Britain was resort entertainment. As Pertwee (1979) describes, beach entertainment in the nineteenth century was given by small groups of minstrels facing a 'ring':

> ... a low boarded enclosure like a circus ring with a small entrance for the patrons. Of course many people would stand outside the ring or sit up on the promenade wall rather than pay their pennies for stepping over the two-foot high barrier. The situation had to be countered and so 'bottling' was introduced. One member of the company, or perhaps two, who were not engaged on the 'platform' if there was one (in many cases there wasn't) would circulate amongst the bystanders outside the ring and collect what they could. A good bottler was worth his weight in gold. The 'bottle' was introduced because once the money had dropped into it, it was virtually impossible to get it out again until the bottle was broken in front of the whole troupe at the end of the performance.

In the 1890s the minstrels were superseded by the small pierrot troupes. It was not until the 1920s that the larger companies began to eat up the smaller – there were still small pierrot troupes on Britain's holiday beaches after the Second World War – and not until the 1950s did resort entertainment become completely intermingled with the rest of the 'entertainment industry'.

Each area of the commercial arts world tends now to be controlled by oligarchic groupings of large 'chain' enterprises. In the terms discussed above (p.34) their managements tend to be unitary, and their senior workforce entrepreneurially oriented. Publishing, which once consisted of hundreds of separate publishing houses and thousands of eccentrically inefficient bookshops, now consists for the most part of vast publishing conglomerates into which older houses were sucked during the eighties (Reed International took over Octopus, which had taken over Secker & Warburg and Mitchell Beazley; Random bought Bodley Head, Cape, Hutchinson and Century). Retail chains (Waterstones, Hatchards, W.H. Smith) between them threaten to obliterate the smaller bookshops.

Pop music, Britain's third largest export earner, accounting for 20% of worldwide CD sales, is similarly controlled 'top down' by a powerful oligarchy of CD producers. In the case of both publishing and CD production, however, new technology (desk-top publishing, interactive CD units) and the increasing difficulty of enforcing the laws of copyright in such new technological realms, mean that there are continuous opportunities for small-scale entrepreneurs to work commercially 'bottom up'.

Grass-roots developments are, however, often seen as a threat by both the civic authorities and by established commercial entrepreneurs. A survey by the Henley Centre for Forecasting (1993) described a huge growth in 'raves' (all night musical parties). More than one million young people were reported to be attending raves each week, spending on average £35.00 at each event. Licensed raves, without any established administrative structure, had become a £2 billion-a-year industry, the same size as the books or newspaper market in Britain. If the unlicensed raves are taken into account, this unofficial 'industry' was probably twice as large. This alarmed both the civic authorities (worried among other things by the high incidence of drug usage reported at the gatherings) and the official Leisure Industry. As the survey said: 'They pose a significant **threat to spending** for sectors such as licensed drink retailers and drinks companies.' (Our emphasis.)

A stranger cultural phenomenon was the fact that in June 1993 it cost the authorities half a million pounds to prevent a cultural festival, which had been organized in Somerset by 'New Age Travellers', from taking place at all. A spokesman said that one of the reasons for banning it was that it would 'attract the wrong kind of people, and harm the tourist industry.'

There are still heroic arts administrators who succeed in presenting opera, major concerts and 'spectacles' on a wholly commercial basis. Harvey Goldsmith, for example, presented Barbra Streisand at the Wembley Arena in 1994 for four performances. Tickets were priced from £48.50 for restricted-view seats to £260 for the best. The 40 000 available seats were sold within a day of going on sale, amounting to some £6.7 million gross receipts (the profits from this one show could, it was argued at the time, pay the subsidy on all four London major orchestras for some years).

Such examples of modern showmanship may serve to remind us of two old showman's maxims: 'Everybody wants to go with the crowd!' and 'The more you charge, the more they want!' A fortnight after going on sale tickets for Ms Streisand's concert were reported to be changing hands for £3000. A fellow impresario, Ed Bicknell, wryly remarked:

In 1992 Dire Straits played to 68 000 at Woburn Abbey, with ticket prices set at £21.50 each. We took a gross of £1.5 million of which all but £12 000 went on overheads, leaving about £1000 each for the band and management. We sometimes don't charge the prices we should! There is a feeling that gigs are to promote loyalty and build a long-term relationship with the fans rather than make money.

The 'mixed service'

In his memoirs the great circus showman 'Lord' George Sanger (1926) recalls a time when he and his travelling circus encountered a toll bridge but had not the money to pay for all their many wagons to cross. Undeterred, he set up his circus, whipped up a local audience, gave an impromptu show by the roadside and made enough money to pay for their crossing.

It is an attractive story, but such bravado ceased to be legally possible when (as we describe in detail in the next chapter) the net of civic legislation gradually closed upon the commercial arts administrator. Copyright law, complex licensing legislation and taxation in particular combined to corral the heady entrepreneurial worlds of Sanger and Barnum and tame them. The administrative world of C.B. Cochran, the great theatre impresario of the twenties and thirties, or of his contemporary Bertram Mills, was much more constrained. This did not prevent either of them from continuing to organize their large-scale undertakings with great skill. C.B. Mills (1985), Bertram Mills' son, who took over the Bertram Mills circus management with his brother, discusses in his memoirs the economics of their annual indoor circus presentation at London's Olympia:

The Grand Hall at Olympia is little more than an ugly shell when a tenant enters it. In our case for every £1000 spent in producing our annual circus about £300 went in building the seating and the stables, decorating them, shutting out the daylight from the glass roof with a sort of red and green bunting 'big top' and generally turning the shell into a comfortable circus building, warm and free from draughts in mid-winter.

For the rest, about 20% was spent on advertising and publicity, about 14% on rent and rates, some 15% on wages and overheads, about 5% on light and heating and only about 14% on artistes' salaries; animal food and odds and ends accounted for about 2%.... To fill 7000 seats twice or three times a day during the first three weeks was easy, but to have full or well-attended matinees when the school holidays were over was a different matter.

Nevertheless, their circus was under increasing pressure: legislation grew ever tighter, costs rose inexorably, and competition became fiercer. The circus broke even in the thirties if it sold only 50% of seats. In the post-war period the break-even point was 75%. Their first post-war Olympia circus made a profit of £211 000. When they decided to close their operation in 1966 the profit was down to £25 000. The Mills brothers felt constricted: the administration had become in their own words 'almost impossibly complicated.'

Such constriction is the mark of this third administrative category: 'mixed' administration in our terms is when a professional administrator is working commercially but within the restraints of extensive government legislation, and in a market considerably shaped by government intervention.

The planned

The main characteristic of planned arts administration is that the professional involved is working to meet some perceived public need, or working to fulfil a prescriptive plan calling for a supply of art. Instead of standing between art and audience, the administrator (or bureaucrat) more usually stands between the prime funding body and the artist. The organization is almost always utilitarian rather than normative in character, and the arts administrators involved have characteristically to deal with more overseer constituencies – which become as important as the external ones, with a corresponding loss of freedom.

Planned arts administration was witnessed in Britain from the middle of the nineteenth century, and soon the effects of planning could be widely seen. New civic halls, art schools and galleries, libraries and museums appeared in provincial cities, and, led in large measure by the Consort, demand grew for national museums and galleries in London. Such provision was held to be answering the deep needs of the populace, but the planned provision was not always greeted with open arms, as a parliamentary speech by William Cobbett (1833) attests:

> He would ask of what use, in the wide world, was this British museum, and to whom, to what class of persons, was it useful? He found that £1000 had been laid out in insects; and surely Hon Members would not assert that these insects were of any use to the ploughboys of Hampshire and of Surrey, and to the weavers of Lancashire! It did a great deal of good to the majority of those who went to it, but to nobody else. The ploughman and the weavers – the shopkeepers and the farmers – never went near it; they paid for it though, whilst the idle loungers enjoyed it, and scarcely paid anything ... Why should tradesmen and farmers be called upon to pay for the support of a place which was intended only for the amusement of the curious and rich, and not for the benefit or for the instruction of the poor?

Well aware of the dangers of prescriptive planning, the British Arts Council in its early years professed a policy of response. They would respond to the local initiative, and respond to the created art, but 'our policy is to have no policy'. Yet, in practice, such a stance proved difficult if not impossible to maintain. Quite soon, the Arts Council was discerning 'needs' on the flimsiest evidence, and, in spite of itself, acting prescriptively to give people what they ought to have wanted, and were thought therefore to need.

A salutary case study from the Council's early years was the failure of the planned West Riding Theatre. This enterprise, wholly subsidized by the Arts Council, at first working between Halifax, Huddersfield and Wakefield, and later substituting Oldham for Wakefield, opened in July 1946 only to close for lack of support the following December. Johns (1947) explores some aspects of the planning that went wrong:

> Perhaps the Arts Council did introduce the scheme on a slightly 'high tone'. As a Halifax authoress remarked to me, 'at first it did seem rather imposed from above'. Certainly it seemed a mistake to have the opening press conference at Leeds, in no way a focal point for the towns concerned. On the other hand, representatives were sent out to investigate audience possibilities in the three towns before the scheme started. Apparently the welfare and personnel departments they contacted in the mills made polite promises – and left it at that. These scouts did not communicate with the local press, which seems rather a pity.
>
> The falling off of 'organised support' after the scheme's first three months deserves mention. Such support included various amateur dramatic societies, whose members would of course have less free time during the Winter. However I think there is something in Mr Toyne's comment: 'when they knew our season was continuing they assumed it to have achieved success and gave up organising parties to support us. It thus appears that the parties were more a duty than a pleasure!

It is hard to rid such activities of the feeling that attending them is indeed a duty rather than a pleasure. Many heavily-subsidized, politically-correct events still have that aura. One reason is that as arts councils have grown in size they have often hijacked the language of the arts, so that only those activities receiving state sponsorship are described as serious 'art'. Expert judgement by people who primarily understand economics and business has been blurred with the critical judgement of those who understand art. Expedient practices, such as the form of deficit funding adopted in its earliest years by the Arts Council of Great Britain, are elevated to the status of principles. And, as the language of arts funding becomes increasingly wrapped in the jargon of social engineering, attending some state-aided arts events is presented as a duty for the socially-progressive, rather than a popular delight.

To use this blurred new language is as destructive of truth and debate as the use of any other political terminology. As a result, the arts administrator who wishes to engage in real discussion has to veer delicately between terminologies borrowed from critical theory, art history, economics, sociology and management studies. This insistent new language may also blind us to the fact that, for all its apparent growth, the state-supported sector of the arts is usually much smaller, and certainly of less overriding importance, than it seems.

The mega-corporate

Alongside the growth of state funding of the arts has been an even more spectacular growth in large entertainment corporations. These organizations have usually been led initially by one charismatic leader, have usually grown rapidly, extending their interests both internationally and across a wide range of services, and have evolved a strong corporate identity which permeates a tightly-structured administration. As with the High Street shops, which seem to represent a large number of small independent businesses, but 95% of which are in fact owned by six major groups, so in the entertainment business the public may not always be aware of how extensive are the holdings, under various names, of the large entertainment corporations. Pearson, for example, which made £208.6 million profit in the year up to December 1993, now owns a Californian computer company *Software Toolworks*, *Penguin* publishers, *Royal Doulton* china, *Chateau Latour* wine, the *Financial Times* and the television production company *Thames Television*.

The best known of all such mega-corporate institutions is the US Disney Corporation, which through its films and videos does business in almost every country in the world. Control of the manufacture and sales of Disney merchandise remains strictly within the corporation, and in its theme parks all the ancillary services (transport, hotels, restaurants and sales) are also owned and operated by it.

Overall, the Disney Corporation is massively profitable, with a balance sheet which resembles that of a sizeable Third World country. Its administrative organization remains rigidly hierarchical, with standardized procedures and a detailed and utilitarian system of control over its staff (staff can be sacked for not smiling enough, but promotion is relatively rapid and pay prospects excellent for ambitious Disney workers who can overcome that hurdle). It retains a highly qualified legal staff to defend its ownership and copyright of the Disney characters, Disney products and the Disney management systems, throughout the world.

Such large corporations, whose enterprises have so large an impact upon the economy, inevitably have a complex relationship with national and local government. When Disney began planning its theme park in Anaheim, a suburb of Los Angeles, in 1985, it invested some £2 billion in the project. The local community was enthusiastic. The main highway was blocked off by the local council and a diversion built from it to accommodate the expected traffic. When the plan was announced Anaheim had 2000 residents and 100 hotel rooms. Now it has a population of 285 000, and 14 000 hotel rooms. Such power gives the Disney corporation confidence to demand that the local council now put up £500 million towards building two huge car parks by the park, which will help to accommodate the ten million visitors expected every year.

Such grand enterprises do not always succeed. EuroDisney, the theme park built by the corporation just outside Paris, failed to attract the expected numbers of visitors, and soon lost heavily. In 1990 a plan to convert the former *Queen*

Mary into a floating theme park, Port Disney, also came to grief. Yet the corporation is so large it can carry such occasional failures. Disney's recent animated film *Aladdin*, not only a huge box office success, but then the bestselling video of all time, soon made more in profits than was lost in the *Queen Mary* débâcle.

The growth of the entertainment corporations carries dangers and benefits, both in the economic and cultural senses. The economics of such large-scale ventures invite large-scale crime, and Knoedelseder (1986) has, for example, described the involvement of the Mafia in the American record business. The involvement of gangland bosses in the vast entertainment centre of Las Vegas has also frequently been described. Yet, at the other end of the scale, the money involved is sometimes ploughed back into the arts in unexpected ways. To take one instance, the owners of the vast *Circus Circus* and *Excalibur* hotels in Las Vegas recently built and opened a third. This is the *Luxor*, a 30-storey black glass pyramid with its own sphinx, containing 2528 rooms. There is a 'museum' with reproductions, and a gift shop where you can buy a seventh-century bronze statue for £10 000. However, there are also serious lectures on Egyptian art and the Egyptian music and dancing shows employ more than 300 professional performers in a year. The hotel chain subsidizes publications which deal with matters of Egyptology, and sells scrolls containing genuine Egyptian calligraphy and painted hieroglyphics. There are also classes in this art. As we shall have occasion to notice below, the world of art and the world of the theme park often curiously interrelate.

REFERENCES

Arts Council of Great Britain (1991) *Participation in the Arts and Crafts.*
Barnard, R. (1913) *The Life and Times of Richard Barnard, Marionette Proprietor.*
Hardy, T. (1886) *The Mayor of Casterbridge.*
Henley Centre for Forecasting (1993) '*Raves*'.
Johns, M. (1947) 'The theatre in the West Riding of Yorkshire', in *Dobson's Theatre Year Book 1947.*
Knoedelseder, W. (1986) *Stiffed: a true story of MCA, the Music Business and the Mafia.*
Marshall, A. (1990) *Sunshine and Laughter.*
Mills, C.B. (1985) *Bertram Mills Circus.*
Murdin, L. (1993) '*The Amateur Operatics*, in *Arts Management Weekly* (Oct., 1993).
National Federation of Women's Institutes (1989 ff.) *The Villages of Britain.*
Pertwee, W. (1979) *Piers and Pierrots.*
Pick, J. (1983) *The West End: Mismanagement and Snobbery.*
Pick, J. (1985) *The Theatre Industry.*
Sanger, G. (1926) *Seventy Years A Showman.*
Thackeray, W.M. (1847–48) *Vanity Fair.*
The London Standard (1985) 'The Londoner Survey'.
Trevelyan, R. (1959) *An Illustrated Social History of England.*

The context

4.1 CULTURAL HISTORY

Comparisons between arts administration techniques in different countries are often too glibly made. It has been a familiar sight for several decades to see tables such as the following, which first appeared in the US *Saturday Review* (22 April, 1972):

Table 4.1 Per capita support for the arts in selected countries

Country	Per capita support ($)
West Germany	2.42
Austria	2.00
Sweden	2.00
Canada	1.40
Israel	1.34
Great Britain	1.23
United States	0.15

Usually the countries which spend less per capita on the arts are held to be demonstrating their philistinism. However, as Schuster (1988) points out, even in purely economic terms such tables offer a misleading and flawed comparison. Only the most visible arts funding agencies are counted, and such studies neglect to account appropriately for the financial support to the arts embedded in foregone taxes. In wider terms they are even more seriously flawed. For 'the arts' are differently defined in each country, with complex attitudes towards each segment of them from different parts of differently-structured populations. Moreover, in such tables 'support' is too readily assumed *only* to consist of state aid.

It could more plausibly be argued that a state with a weak education system, with strong censorship, a poor transport infrastructure and which imposes heavy taxation and a burdensome series of legal obligations upon the arts should not be complimented just because its per capita 'support' for the arts appears to be high. Such high spending can be a sign of weakness, not strength. In such a country, state aid may be high because, without it, the arts could barely survive at all. When general socioeconomic conditions are better, state aid is arguably needed less.

State aid is therefore only one of many factors which together form the cultural and socioeconomic context in which the arts administrator works. There are many others: the general level of education, the existing levels of participation in the arts, the legal systems of licensing and censorship, the country's wealth, its distribution and the taxation systems are among them. But, perhaps, the most important of all is the country's *Zeitgeist*, the prevailing attitude towards freedom, ideas, convention, laughter, revolution, order and change.

4.2 THE CONSTRAINTS OF HISTORY

The task of administering the arts differs according to each country's history. The obvious matters such as the nature of the country's cultural heritage, the disposition of its population, the history and quality of its general education system, and the general distribution of wealth, profoundly affect the kind of aesthetic contracts the arts administrator can make. A French person does not visit the Comédie Française with the same assumptions, attitudes and expectations as a Russian visiting the Taganka, and the arts administrator needs to know a great deal more about both than the fact they are 'theatregoers'.

Cultural history shapes the frame of reference differently for theatregoers in different countries: it also shapes the different ways in which people in different countries look at paintings, interpret dance, understand poetry and even the way they hear music. Sometimes, the differences are clear. We acknowledge that some British comedians flop on Broadway because they have a 'British sense of humour', for instance. We may be more surprised when a serious film is liked in one country but not in another, or when it becomes clear that the Elgin Marbles mean something quite different to Greeks than to the British. And, some British people are indignant when they learn that Muslim fundamentalists are so offended by the contents of Salman Rushdie's novel *The Satanic Verses* that a *fatwa*, a sentence of death, has been passed upon him.

Yet we should not perhaps be surprised that different religions, different regions and different countries with their divergent cultural attitudes react in such radically different ways and draw radically different meanings from the same work of art. If the arts actually were (as some planners and bureaucrats have insisted) simply a 'product like any other' then it would indeed be surprising. But an art work, as we have stressed earlier (Introduction, and Chapter 1 above), is not simply a product with a fixed value to be bought and sold. Art does not exist until it has been understood by and benefited its audience. The understanding of an audience is an integral part of art, and as that understanding varies, so the reception accorded to an artist's work will vary. It is to be expected therefore that an art work will sometimes be thought excellent in one country but bad in another, or even that an art work in one culture is not seen as art anywhere else.

Each of us finds it difficult fully to understand and benefit from an art work which clearly belongs to a culture quite different from our own. Sometimes we can make a successful transition, placing ourselves within another culture sufficiently to understand at least intellectually what a sitar recital means to cultivated Indians, or a traditional Noh drama means to the Japanese. An Arab may similarly be able to make the intellectual effort to look at a Stubbs painting, and see the horses through British eyes. But our capacity to make such cultural adaptations is limited, and it is limited largely by language.

Cultural attitudes are embedded in language, which is 'the pillar of group identity' (Edwards, 1985). All forms of colonialism, including cultural colonialism, attempt to impose 'official' languages, but many hundreds of minority languages seem remarkably resilient. In Nigeria, for example, the 80 million inhabitants speak about 400 languages. On the Pacific island of Vanuatu 100 000 people still speak more than a hundred languages despite having French and English as their two official languages. Even in London more than 140 languages are spoken. This is of central importance to the arts administrator.

Our languages shape our thoughts, attitudes and understanding. Even when watching or listening to performances which apparently transcend language – dance programmes, or concerts – or when looking at something which contains no words – a tapestry, or finely woven carpet – we still cannot escape the constrictions of language. A Finlander does not hear the music of Sibelius in quite the same way as a Greek, and a Turk does not see a silken carpet in quite the same way as an American. Even when the art is not conveyed in language, its understanding is inevitably shaped by the language of its audience. So the arts administrator must be sensitive to language – both everyday language, which enshrines people's attitudes and reactions, and the more specialist language of critical dialogue. Without a keen ear for the way people talk, the arts administrator cannot fully understand the cultural context in which he or she is attempting to work, and, more practically, cannot explain or advertise the arts to a particular public (a point we elaborate in Chapter 7 below).

4.3 LEGAL CONSTRAINTS

Governments impose many restraints on venues and on performances, as well as legal curbs on the populace and their right to assemble as audiences. We return to these matters of licensing in Chapter 5. For the moment we are concerned with the legal constraints on artists and art.

When there is any general curtailment of the freedom of expression, in print or speech, artists will be affected. For example, the fact that matters due to come before the courts in Britain may not be publicly discussed – the principle of *sub judice* – can lead to legal action being taken against an artist, as occurred in 1994 when an injunction was served on a London management intending to present *Maxwell – the Musical*.

There is in Britain, as elsewhere, a long history of direct legal restraint on artists and the public presentation of works of art. Before the *Theatres Act 1968* abolished direct theatre censorship, the Lord Chamberlain's office, for more than two centuries, effectively had had powers to license or forbid any kind of performance on a British stage. The British theatre was thus censored much more strictly than other art forms, which occasionally led to such absurdities as the moment in Peter Brook's 1963 Aldwych production of *US* when the auditorium lights were raised so that the audience could read a poem, printed in the programme, which the Lord Chamberlain had forbidden to be spoken on stage. That kind of anomaly ended with the 1968 Act which, in place of that censorship, created three specific offences regarding the performance of plays: obscenity, incitement to racial hatred and provoking a breach of the peace.

The offence of obscenity as defined in the Act is similar to that spelt out in the *Obscene Publications Acts* of 1959 and 1964, which cover novels, poetry and painting: 'an article shall be deemed to be obscene if its effect is, taken as a whole, such as to tend to deprave and corrupt persons who are likely, having regard to all relevant circumstances, to read, see, or hear the matter contained or embodied in it.' The tautology of this attempted definition is made even less effective by the Act's later statement that an art work can be defended if it 'is justified as being for the public good on the ground that it is in the interests of science, literature, art or learning, or of other objects of general concern.' (As no definition of 'art' appears in law, the courts may be helped, at their discretion, by 'experts'.)

The offences of incitement to racial hatred and of provoking a breach of the peace exist when the performance, taken as a whole, is deemed to be doing this. There is one crucial difference, however, between the way the law operates for the publication of books (etc.) and the presentation of stage performances. No proceedings can be brought against a stage presentation without the consent of the Attorney-General, but proceedings may be brought against books or other publications without that restriction.

A further crucial area in which the artist is constrained by law is within the area of defamation by libel or slander. The distinction between these two is in the form the defamation takes: if it is spoken it is slander, and if published in a more permanent form, libel. The distinction is not always clear. For example, the *Defamation Act 1952* ordains that the broadcasting of words by television and radio is to be considered as publication in permanent form, and in this context 'words' include pictures, visual images, gestures and other methods of signifying meaning. The exact status of film, CDs, records, video tapes and the like is less clear. The visual material of film is plainly to be considered as publication in a permanent form, and hence as potential libel, but the sound track of film (or video or other recordings) may somewhat confusingly be classed as spoken defamation, and hence slander.

Defining 'defamation' causes as much difficulty as does the definition of obscenity. The classical definition is an utterance 'which tends to lower the injured party in the estimation of right-thinking members of society' but in a society of highly confused values, and in which there is no clear way of knowing who are the right-thinking members of society, that is little assistance. As a consequence, there have been many and varied lawsuits for 'defamation' of character in publications and in the media. It is hardly possible to lay down clear guidelines, as the results of such cases have been so spectacularly varied, but it is worth setting down the permitted defences against defamation of character:

- **Justification** is a sufficient defence if the utterance can be shown to have been true.
- **Qualified privilege** is a defence used when reporting public meetings (providing the plaintiff has been given opportunity to explain or contradict the report) and when reporting comments made by a public official in the course of his duty.
- **Fair comment** is a defence when the matter treated upon is a cause of genuine public concern.

The guiding question must always be that of justification, of whether the utterance was true or not. This may be difficult to resolve, as 'truth' is less clear in art than it is made to appear in the courtroom – much of the meaning in art depends upon context and the way in which allusions may be understood. A straightforwardly untrue statement, however, may not be defended on other grounds. When a London theatrical management presented Rolf Hochhuth's controversial play *Soldiers* it was no defence for them to say that the subject matter – Churchill's alleged involvement in a plot to kill the Polish Prime Minister Gerald Sikorski – was a cause of genuine public concern, because they were found guilty of the libel of untruthfully saying that the pilot of the plane which crashed and killed the General was implicated in the plot. (Unlike Churchill the pilot was still alive, and so able to bring the action.)

It is important for arts administrators to understand that in British law managements (of theatres, concert halls or galleries) are, like newspaper proprietors and printers, equally responsible with the actual author for any proven defamation. Intermediaries, and those with a subordinate role in its dissemination (singers, actors, cinema box office staff, bookshop assistants, for instance) are not liable if they are innocent of the defamation.

4.4 FINANCIAL CONSTRAINTS

An arts administrator needs to know as much as possible about a potential audience. One key factor in planning and pricing an arts programme (Chapters 7 and 8 below) is the disposable income that each section of that audience has, coupled with the cost to them of such things as safe transport to and from the venue, parking, babysitters, or a meal after the show. Unfortunately, there is no ready way of acquiring this kind of information. It is possible to find out, in broad terms, the incomes of various bands within the potential audience, but not easy to adduce from that what their disposable income might be. When some kind of figure for disposable income has been arrived at, then it is still not easy to price admissions to arts events, as they may be well down the list of people's spending priorities. Nor is it easy to tabulate the additional costs involved for different kinds of people travelling to an arts event. Some are happy to take public transport, while others want to take cars. Some want to 'make' the evening with a drink and a meal, but others do not.

Yet we must use all available figures. We could, for example, begin by looking at the *General Household Survey 1992* which gives us the figures for gross weekly income in Britain by family type:

Table 4.2 Gross family income in Britain by family type

Family type		Usual gross weekly income			
		£0–150	£150–250	£250–350	£350/over
Married couple	%	11	13	17	59
Lone mother	%	63	18	9	11
Single	%	65	12	8	12
Widowed	%	28	28	16	28
Divorced	%	59	24	9	9
Separated	%	67	17	8	9

Such information may at times be useful in itself, but until we know much more about the circumstances of each 'family type' it is insufficient to start planning a pricing structure. One particular difficulty we face is that the 'black economy' by which people earn unrecorded sums 'moonlighting' is unknown to the statisticians. Some, though by no means the majority, may be somewhat better off than the official statistics show them to be. Many may be worse off, because they have additional family demands on their resources, live in expensive accommodation, or are in debt. Of overarching significance is the relative ease with which credit may be obtained.

There is considerable evidence that many of the audience who pay high prices to attend pop concerts, for example, cannot strictly speaking 'afford' to do so. Yet the event has such high priority that the ticket is bought 'on credit', even if it means doing without essentials, or going into debt. It is thus always of great interest to look at spending on 'inessentials', such as CD players, which people nevertheless think are of great importance to their lives. The following table shows the high importance British people give, whatever their income level, to the purchase of such 'inessentials':

Table 4.3 Ownership of media equipment

% households with:	1972	1982	1987	1992
Television Colour	–	77	86	96
Black and white	–	20	12	3
All TV	93	97	98	99
Video recorder	0	0	31	72
CD player	0	0	0	33
Home computer	0	0	13	23
Telephone	42	76	81	89

These figures indicate that the problem with live arts events is probably not that they are priced too highly, but that they are thought to be of less value than the music and soap operas which technology brings into the home. After all, few tickets for arts events cost as much as a video recorder.

Discussion of leisure spending opens up the whole question of the effects of tax upon arts organizations. One effect is plainly that an increase in tax is likely to cut box office income. The reverse however is not necessarily true. When between 1983 and 1993 taxes in Britain were reduced, there was no noticeable increase in box office spending. Instead, the British spent their additional income, in part, on having more overseas holidays. As a result, Britain's balance of payments on its tourist account sank from a deficit of just over £1 billion in 1983 to a monumental £3.4 billion in 1993. It would seem that lower taxes, coupled with high state subsidies for arts events, meant that the cultivated classes could spend more time and money overseas.

Increased local taxes, which in Britain are based on the occupation of property, currently termed the 'community charge', seem to achieve something of the same result. An increase tends to have a harmful effect on leisure spending, but a decrease does not necessarily increase local spending on the arts (in part because people save up to take more holidays away from home). Moreover, when government taxation on goods and services, Britain's long-established purchase tax and the more recent value-added tax, is increased, it has a double effect on arts organizations. They will almost certainly have to pay more in tax, and their potential audiences have less to spend at the box office, because they too have had to pay the additional tax.

It is, however, extremely difficult to create a context in which the taxation system works favourably for the arts. When governments offer tax breaks to one part of the leisure industry they usually have to make up for the revenue they have foregone by taxing another. For example, in 1986 when the French

National Assembly gave local museums tax breaks on arts grants and private donations, they recouped their lost tax revenue by a further increase in VAT on pornographic films, cassettes and magazines. Likewise, when governments simultaneously reduce taxation and grant aid, it is generally less acceptable to arts organizations because there is no guarantee that the additional spending will be in the arts. It is more difficult to target tax incentives than grant aid.

4.5 SUPPORT SYSTEMS

Most accounts of support systems in a country target only the most obvious ones: the direct aid given to arts organizations by national and local governments, and the direct aid given by government quangos (Introduction, above) and by trusts and foundations. In Britain these are of great importance, but one must forget neither the less obvious sources of direct aid – the Armed Forces' support of music, the Queen's art collection, the fostering of the arts by the Church – nor the indirect support given to the arts by the state education system, the state library service and by private philanthropy.

We are here concerned with the context of the arts administrator's work, and the first point that must be made is that there is no one system of support for arts organizations. The present authors have for example argued (1989) that, excluding support from the Royal Family and from the churches, there were twenty-four clearly defined different 'models' of arts support still operating in Britain.

The interlocking systems are complex, and gaining up-to-date information about them is a daunting task for a working arts administrator. There are three consequences of this. The first is that 'fund raising' has become a specialism in itself within the arts administration framework. The second is that arts organizations have increasingly to purchase information about support systems from the growing numbers of specialist agencies, who now occupy a powerful place within the arts bureaucracy. The third is that, because the administrative unit in an arts organization has to acquire knowledge of, and make applications for, an increasingly wide range of grant-aid support, the bureaucracy involved in each organization has increased prodigiously.

Arts organizations in Britain have to try to acquire grant aid from many sources (local, regional, national and European). They have also to accommodate the fact that these are increasingly interdependent (grant aid on capital building projects for example is now rarely given until the organization can show that it has made satisfactory revenue funding arrangements for operating the building when work is done), and they are interwoven by 'matching grant' systems. Overall, the 'mixed funding' system government has encouraged in Britain since 1979 has undoubtedly had the effects of greatly increasing the size of the arts bureaucracy, increasing the specialisms within it, and of compartmentalizing the information on which it depends.

Britain has followed the United States in its encouragement of business support for the arts. The British body which acts as a go-between, encouraging and developing links between the arts and the commercial world, is the Association for Business Sponsorship in the Arts (ABSA). It was set up in 1976, a decade after Rockefeller had initiated a similar business committee for the arts in the US.

It took some little time to re-establish the notion of business sponsorship in the British arts world (p.84 below). ABSA's first estimate of total business support for the arts in Britain was only £600 000. By 1986 however that estimate had risen to £25 million, and by 1993 was estimated at £58 million (a fall of 13.5% from a 'high' in the previous year). ABSA had itself begun to diversify its activities, opening regional offices, an advisory service called 'Business in the Arts' (300 volunteers giving free business advice to volunteers all over the country), and a service helping arts organizations create business strategies (for which there is a fee).

The most decisive step in integrating the activities of ABSA and those of government arts planners was taken in 1984 with the creation of the Business Sponsorship Incentive Scheme (BSIS), again based on a successful American operation. Under that scheme government doubles the money newly put in to the arts by the business community. This has been a considerable success: in its first year BSIS raised £1 million, but the total a decade later exceeded £75 million.

Yet the bureaucracy of the 'mixed funding' system, the fact that some 'high profile' arts organizations are plainly more attractive to commercial sponsors than others, and the widespread feeling that the system favours the larger arts organizations with big administrative staffs, still cause some doubts about the context in which arts administrators must now work to secure grant aid. However, much less is now heard of an old worry, that the commercial sponsors will directly interfere with the artists' and the programmers' freedom. Many people would agree with the artistic director of the Royal Shakespeare Company, Adrian Noble (1993), who emphasized that it had not happened and would never happen with his company:

> Since business started cautiously sniffing towards the arts world and the arts community started shyly looking towards marriage, there has been consistent growth both in terms of cash delivered and also confidence ... no sponsor ever has, or ever will, interfere with our artistic policy. When we seek a sponsor we seek one for whom that policy will shine.

4.6 ADMINISTRATIVE TRADITIONS

Until 1979, two administrative traditions informed the British system of running its national cultural organizations. The first was the 'arm's length' principle –

the convention by which government voted money in support of the organization's work but kept 'at arm's length' from the organization's decisions about spending it. The second, the 'peer group' principle, was a consequence of the first: it was that organizational decisions about spending should be made by those working in, or who were highly knowledgeable about, the field of benefit, the 'peers' of those supported by government funds.

Thus organizations such as the BBC, the British Council and, later, the Arts Council of Great Britain were run by boards or councils whose members were not elected politicians but people experienced in, or with a deep interest in, the work of the organization. There was a bi-partisan notion of 'public service', which animated these realms of public life.

Those asked to serve came from a notional list of suitable persons who had usually distinguished themselves in public life. They were sometimes called 'the great and the good'. Inevitably they were rather middle-of-the-road, rather elderly people with sufficient paid leisure to undertake the tasks required of them. Some disliked this 'old boy/old girl' network, and there were calls for the Arts Council at any rate to be reconstituted as an elected body (Jenkins, 1977).

In the event such arguments soon appeared inconsequential, for such mandarin conventions as the 'arm's length' principle disappeared in the much more fundamental changes in administrative context. Notions of public service were submerged in a revolution in public attitudes.

A large number of people became persuaded that all areas of public life must be planned, and accounted for, in purely economic terms. Health, education and the social services were urged to regard themselves less as state services than as industrial units 'delivering' their wares to 'clients'. The cultural life of the nation was now often termed 'the arts industry'. The British Council was urged to rethink its activities so that it could deliver 'value for money' in its promotion of art.

Perhaps the greatest change however was in the widespread adoption of businesslike 'policies' for culture, so that the British adopted the kind of prescriptive two, three or four year development 'planning' which they had earlier professed to find objectionable in totalitarian regimes. This was a vast attitudinal change. The word 'policy' had formerly meant 'deceit' or 'trickery' (British governments in the early nineteenth century, significantly enough, only had foreign 'policies'). For decades having government 'arts policies' had been as unthinkable in Britain as state arranged marriages, but, by the mid-eighties, all political parties seemed to have decided, as a necessary part of the prevailing commercial climate, that the British state should plan for the arts.

The well-established British public traditions of arts administration could not be so easily dispensed with. Politicians, no less than artists and arts administrators, have continued to give at any rate token support for the arm's length principle and peer group assessment. Moreover, although an ever-swelling arts bureaucracy talked a tough new 'managerial' language, and seemed to be attempting to ride roughshod over the feelings of artists and arts administrators, it was noteworthy that in numerous confrontations between the prescriptive new state bureaucracy and the practitioners – threats to withdraw theatre funding from the provinces, rows over the future of several major festivals, or Dance Umbrella, or in the long-running row over London's orchestras – it was almost always state officialdom which was forced to back down. Although it is not formally enshrined in any legal or firm organizational form, the fellow-feeling of artists and arts administrators can be a powerful force, for its traditions are of far longer standing than any transitory political/economic movement.

It will thus be clear that pressures of very different kinds bear upon the administrator, or administration team. In dealing with each of them, an arts administrator must always bear in mind the effects of any decision upon the others. A new legal requirement will have financial implications. A political change will equally clearly affect every part of the context in which the administrator works. Unless this is fully understood, a modern arts organization is in constant danger of being torn apart by the differing demands now made upon it by its various constituencies.

One of the major requirements of an arts administrator is that he or she should be able to think of their work as being what we later define as **holistic** management. Each person involved, though with specialist tasks to perform, must be aware that each of their actions reflects upon the specialized work of every other person. Equally importantly, the arts administrator, or team, must generate a general acceptance by each part of the organization that everything which happens to another specialized area will have repercussions for their own work. This ability of an arts administrator is more easily recognized over time than analysed in textbook detail, but certainly involves:

- considerable communication skills;
- a readiness to 'personalize' the organization and give it a unifying, readily understood, character;
- an ability to foster a strong organizational memory, so that all its members know the past successes of the organization and the beliefs and practices which nourished them.

Although all arts administrators work within the same administrative contexts, it can never be too strongly emphasized that arts organizations cannot, for bureaucratic convenience, be standardized. The seat pricing policies of the Glasgow Citizens Theatre, the Chester Gateway and Glyndebourne are, by tradition, quite different. The marketing strategies of the Manchester Hallé, City of Birmingham Symphony and London Philharmonic Orchestras are equally distinct. Attempts to standardize theatre management practice, or to standardize the marketing of orchestras can only result in the gradual destruction of each separate organization, and a loss of its unique character. That is one reason why fostering a lively sense of the uniqueness of each organization is so important, and why the good administrator will be continually at pains to keep proud organizational memories fresh.

REFERENCES

ABSA Annual Report (1993).

Edwards, J. (1985) *Language, Society and Identity.*

General Household Survey (1992).

Jenkins, H. (1977) *The Culture Gap.*

Noble, A. (1993) 'The High Price of Defending that Pound of Flesh', in *The Times* (9 Dec. 1993).

Pick, J. and Anderton, M. (1989) *Industrial Support for the Arts.*

Schuster, Mark D. (1988) 'The search for international models', in *'Who's to pay for the Arts?'* (1988).

5 | Government intervention: supports and constraints

5.1 GOVERNMENT MOTIVES

As Wilson Knight (1962) pointed out, the patron god of the performing arts, Dionysus, has always been an enemy of orderly government: '... he is always threatening it, both with lusts, indecencies and indignities, and with crimes, ghosts and death. There is nothing respectable or civilised about him: he is the enemy of such qualities.' This ancient truth should remind us that the most benign of governments will sometimes even now try to suppress dramas, books and paintings which are Dionysian in spirit: that is, works which seem to them to be morally irresponsible, subversive in thought or an incitement to revolution. Sophocles' *Oedipus Rex*, for example, was thought by the British to be too dangerous for performance in English until the 1930s. Sometimes even music may be suppressed by a government because it seems to be linked with an enemy of the state; thus the music of Wagner (said to be Hitler's favourite composer) is still actively discouraged today in Israel.

A second reason governments have for constraining activity in the arts is an ancient 'fear of the mob'. Popular arts movements tend to alarm the authorities; any large, emotional, easily-swayed gathering at a pop concert, rave or rally raises the spectre of the crowd storming the Winter Palace. So, although we begin this chapter by discussing government support of the arts, we must keep in mind that there are parallel ways in which governments, even as they seem to 'support' the arts, are also striving to constrain it.

Titmuss (1970; 1974) first suggested that the motives of governments apparently acting to benefit their peoples could be readily, if somewhat cynically, categorized. His models, briefly outlined below, give us a useful guide to what government motives may be when they 'support' the arts.

1. The Glory Model

Although 'glory' as a term has fallen into disuse, it is still a useful way of describing the desire of rulers and governments that their time shall be remembered as a golden age, and their regime as civilized and harmonious. Examples: President Mitterand's new Bastille Opera House; the Palace of Culture built in post-war Warsaw.

2. The Placebo Model

Governments may seek to assuage public outrage at some hardship or injustice by offering artistic pleasures to their people. Examples: the US Federal 'Art for the Millions' scheme begun during the great depression; the Urban District Council of Hong Kong's 'People's Opera in the Parks' scheme, begun immediately after the Kowloon Ferry riots.

3. The Education Model

Non-Dionysiac art, which seems to be in accord with official thinking, may sometimes be promoted by governments as a means of educating the populace in correct habits of thought. Examples: the 'Cars of Thespis' movement in Fascist Italy, which took politically correct drama and opera to every community; the regional arts movement in the Third Reich, which employed a massive government force both to promote the politically acceptable and to stamp out cultural activity which was considered potentially revolutionary.

4. The Reward Model

Governments may promote the arts to a group thought to be deserving of them, because of that group's service to the state. Examples: the British government's support of ENSA (Entertainment National Services Association), which took music, drama and other entertainment to the troops during the 1939–45 war; the USSR promotion of the arts in the Steppes, for the conscripted workforce that 'opened up' the formerly barren area.

5. The Service Model

Making a cultural resource widely available and generally accessible means the arts become one of the public services. Examples: the Swedish government's grant-aid to their national newspaper organizations; the Danish government's support for their regional museums.

6. The Compensatory Model

When the support system for a cultural amenity collapses, governments whose actions may have caused the breakdown may sometimes choose, in compensation, to take it over. Examples: the municipal authorities in the German Democratic Republic taking over the running of formerly private opera houses; the Turkish government taking over the running of many archaeological sites, formerly run by foreign foundations.

7. The Commercial Model

Rulers and governments may regard their cultural assets as saleable products, or as economic levers to commercial profit. Examples: the French promotion of their national museums and galleries as tourist attractions (tourism has increased by 50% since the Louvre pyramid opened); the British Royal Family's decision (1993) to open Buckingham Palace as a London visitor attraction.

No country, of course, supports the arts for just one of these reasons. Political motives, like any others, are mixed. Neither is there an obvious correlation between a government's motives for supporting a particular project and the money they give to it. So the familiar economic arguments for government support, which must now be considered, cannot readily be matched with Titmuss' models.

5.2 GOVERNMENT FINANCIAL SUPPORT

The economic arguments for direct government support of the arts can be grouped in three categories.

- *The 'Avant Garde'*: that there must be some public support of an artist's work until public taste has moved sufficiently to support it on the open market.
- *The Cost Disease*: that because the production of art is necessarily labour-intensive, inflation in the arts rises more rapidly than in the rest of the economy, and therefore the arts must be especially assisted.
- *The Economic Impact*: in the micro-economics of arts industries a loss is made, but in the wider macro-economic picture, the arts generate wealth, therefore they should be invested in.

The first argument was used in submissions by many arts councils in the sixties and early seventies. It was a pervasive belief held in its early days by the Arts Council of Great Britain; it was Lord Keynes' feeling that the ultimate aim of state aid was to teach organizations to do without it (Harrod, 1951). It seems however to have been something of a pipe dream. There has been no case in an English-speaking country of any organization which has been receiving grant aid over a period being weaned from it and successfully operating as a purely commercial operation.

The second argument, generally known as the 'cost disease' problem in the sixties and early seventies, was particularly associated with the US economists Baumol and Bowen. As Hilda Baumol and W.J. Baumol (1985) later observed, 'since the cost disease was described in 1964, arts administrators throughout the world have been using the model to back up their requests for increases in government support for the arts.' However, as the Baumols also said, their original description of the 'cost disease' had severe limitations: their model applied only to orchestras, was applicable only within the US economy, and did not apply in periods of inflation. The notion of the differential 'cost disease' was further dented by authoritative research in Britain undertaken by Peacock, Shoesmith and Millner (1983). As Peacock (1993) says:

> Our carefully detailed researches showed, quite unequivocally, that the differential effect of inflation on the performing – sorry – performed –

arts over the period in question (1970–1982) was comparatively slight ... in the case of the London orchestras alone, the average annual change in real costs (after allowing for inflation), actually fell throughout the 1970s and early 1980s.

The third argument is most often used to try to persuade governments that the arts are a major tourist attraction and that without subsidized arts many visitors would not be spending within the economy at all. When discussing tourist spending, the 'arts industry' is usually extended to include all the goods and services associated with participating in or visiting an art event, including transport, catering, hotel services and all spending which takes place incidentally during the trip. The claim is then made that spending generated by an arts event is, usually, about two and a half times the cost of tickets sold for it.

There are four main problems with the 'economic impact' line of argument. First, it is contentious to say that if people were not going to an arts event, they would never choose to dine out, stay in hotels or take taxis. (It is equally fallacious to say that taxation on arts tickets is a special form of arts donation to government; if there were no arts event the customer would probably spend on some other taxed leisure activity and the government would still get the money.) Second, although the arts may attract tourists, they are rarely the only reason for a visit. Third, it could be argued that in a country such as Britain, which makes a huge annual loss on its tourist account, state subsidies to the arts could well allow the well-off to go to the opera relatively cheaply at home so they could spend even more abroad. The fourth objection is that although impact studies may show us that an arts festival, for example, increases spending within a city, it is where the money ends up that matters. Such spending may hardly benefit the local economy or local arts economy at all, but may end up swelling the profits of distant corporations, who own the hotels, restaurants, bars and transport services.

Indeed, as government statisticians are only too well aware, the argument that the arts should be grant-aided as 'investment' because they generate a wider wealth can be turned on its head. It is just as easy to say that it is the tax on the profitable pop music industry which allows government to grant aid other kinds of music. Or, to move to another field, one can look at the contributions made to Britain's balance of trade over a decade by largely commercial UK-produced films at 1992 prices:

Year	£ million
1983	99
1984	104
1985	131
1986	115
1987	147
1988	145
1989	158
1990	179
1991	182
1992	189

These contributions to the British economy are almost as large as the total sum disbursed on the subsidized arts by the Arts Council of Great Britain in each year. (In 1992/3, for instance, the total Arts Council grant was £186 359 000.) So, although it can be argued that in some areas, such as the theatre, commercial organizations benefit from exploiting talent nurtured in the subsidized sector, it could equally be said that the domestic subsidy system is in itself paid for by the profitable overseas trading of British films, television programmes, books and the pop music industry.

It is fair to say, however, that in practice governments do not seem ever to be persuaded by any of these well-worn economic arguments. As virtually every government does, nevertheless, support the arts, it is reasonable to assume that the political models discussed above (5.1) might be a better guide to their motives. This view is supported by the fact that patterns of government support across the world do not vary as much as the different economic systems, and radically changing economic circumstances would suggest they should. Arguments for state support which are couched in economic terms may often reveal themselves as political on closer inspection.

Direct state support is generally given to arts organizations either in the form of a one-off donation (sometimes called an award or a capital grant), usually to assist with setting up or building costs, or in the form of an annual grant. Annual grant aid is usually given to cover an expected loss in the running costs of an arts organization. When it is allied to a particular phase in the organization's work, it is sometimes called a project grant. When it is expected to continue for a long period, it is often referred to as revenue funding.

'Funding' in the arts world is not used in its strict sense (i.e. income deriving from invested funds) but as a general term for 'financial support'. In most countries funding has become very much more complicated in recent years, with straightforward government and local government grant aid running in tandem with 'matching grant' systems (such as the incentive funding scheme mentioned above, pp.59–60). An increasingly interlocked system demands that, for instance, arts organizations have to satisfy funders that they have revenue funding assured before they can be considered for capital grants.

The British grant aid systems are now extremely complicated. Slightly more than half of state funding for the arts in Britain comes from local governments. Tabulating that funding presents its own problems, not the least of which is the eclectic notions of 'the arts' held in different quarters. A local government authority may, for example, be shown to have increased its support of 'the arts' because it has increased its grant aid to a civic theatre, but it may have taken the money from the book purchasing account of the library service (which is not usually included in 'the arts'), so overall may actually be spending less. The following table shows the best available indication (CIPFA Leisure and Recreation Statistics, 1992/3) of current local government spending on the arts in Britain:

Table 5.1 Local government spending on the arts in Britain, 1992/3

	Population '000s	Arts and museums spending £'000s	£ per head
North	3 027	23 708	7.83
North West	6 329	34 611	5.46
Yorks and Humberside	4 837	33 269	6.87
W. Midlands	5 150	35 931	6.97
E. Midlands	3 284	23 732	7.22
Eastern	5 640	34 635	6.14
South West	3 718	14 064	3.78
South	4 470	22 976	5.14
London	6 680	70 541	10.56
South East	3 920	18 846	4.80
England	47 055	312 313	6.63
Scotland	5 111	53 293	10.43
Wales	2 892	13 274	4.59
N. Ireland	1 578	5 246	3.32
UK totals	56 636	384 126	6.78

Central government support for the arts in Britain is disbursed by the new Department of National Heritage, a Ministry which now includes the national collections (libraries, museums and galleries, the Royal Armouries, the government art collection and other cultural property), the built heritage, the living arts, the media (broadcasting, film and the press), sport and recreation, tourism and the National Lottery in its brief. As will be seen, these categories are different from those in local government departmental structure, and they still leave arts organizations having to deal with many other government departments, as well as many neo-governmental organizations, trusts and charities.

In all, the Ministry spends around a billion pounds a year (in 1992/3 £1 008 000 000). Expenditure in 1992/3 in key categories was as follows:

Table 5.2 Dept. National Heritage Central Government expenditures voted in estimates 1992/3

	£
Museums and galleries	211 000 000
Arts (passed to the arts councils)	236 000 000
Libraries	133 000 000
Welsh fourth TV channel	56 000 000
Assistance to films	22 000 000
Tourism	46 000 000
Occupied royal palaces and other historic buildings, historic royal palaces and royal parks agencies	58 000 000
Historic buildings, ancient monuments, royal armouries and national heritage	134 000 000

(In subsequent years the Department made a significant contribution to the European Regional Development Fund.) In 1992/3 the specified arts allocation (£236 000 000) for Britain was distributed as follows:

Table 5.3 Distribution (per head of population) of government funds for the arts

Arts councils	£'000s	£ per head
England	186 359	3.96
Scotland	22 691	4.44
Wales	12 708	4.39
N. Ireland	8 801	5.58
Crafts Council	3 000	
Business Sponsorship Investment Scheme	4 400	
Other arts support	6 900	

In the case of the Arts Council of England, a proportion of its income (more than £40 million in 1992/3) is passed on in the form of grant aid to the ten Regional Arts Boards (RABs). An increasing number of client arts organizations have in recent years been taken out of the central Arts Council's control and passed on to these boards. This three-layered arts bureaucracy aims for a coherent overall strategy by having the RABs prepare three-year forward plans for approval by the central Arts Council, which then reflects RAB plans in its own corporate plan, submitted in turn for approval to the Department of National Heritage.

The Ministry made these allocations from its 1992/3 funds (£211 000 000) to museums and galleries in England:

	£'000s
British Museum	32 400
Imperial War Museum	11 000
National Gallery	17 100
National Maritime Museum	11 600
National Museum of Science and Industry	21 900
National Museums and Galleries on Merseyside	13 400
National Portrait Gallery	5 500
Natural History Museum	28 900
Tate Gallery	16 000
Victoria and Albert Museum	29 300
Wallace Collection	1 900
Geffrye Museum	900
Horniman Museum	2 600
Museums and Galleries Commission	8 800
Museums and Galleries Improvement Fund	1 600
Museum of London	4 100
Museum of Science and Industry in Manchester	2 200
Sir John Soane's Museum	600
Research and support services, including museums	
Training Institute	800
Government Indemnity	400

The Museums and Galleries Commission also partly funds the seven Area Museum Councils in England. The Commission also represents the 2000 or so registered museums and galleries in the UK. (Of these around 1100 are independent, some being supported by local authorities.)

In Britain there are about 5300 public libraries, including small units and mobile libraries, with about 600 libraries in further and higher education, some 5600 school libraries and about 2200 specialized libraries in both the public and the private sector. In 1992/3 local authorities spent a total of £626 500 000 on the public library service in Britain. This was supplemented by the DNH grant of £69 322 000 to the British Library, and a further £58 000 000 to the building of the new British Library at St Pancras. In all, public expenditure on libraries in Britain in a year totals some £1.3 billion, 0.28% of the gross domestic product.

Further small but significant items of grant aid from the Department of National Heritage (1992/3) were:

Table 5.4 Grant aid from the Dept. of National Heritage 1992/3

Institution	£'000s
British Film Institute	15 000
(The BFI has established regional	
BFI centres throughout the UK)	
British Screen Finance	2 000
(BSF is a private sector industry, loaning	
money for low- and medium-budget films)	
National Film and Television School	1 850
Broadcasting Standards Council	1 267
(The BSC draws up codes of practice for all	
publicly-licensed broadcasting in the UK,	
and monitors output)	
British Tourist Authority	30 900
English Tourist Board	16 200

The British Tourist Authority has a general responsibility for the UK and for tourism promotion overseas. In addition to the English Tourist Board, there is a Welsh Tourist Board and a Scottish Tourist Board, funded by the Welsh and Scottish Offices respectively. The BTA and ETA are jointly responsible for the 11 English Regional Tourist Boards.

Even after such a cursory sketch of government grant aid in Britain it will be readily seen that despite efforts to produce coherent 'strategies', administrators of arts centres in particular are likely to have to deal with more than one government department: the Department of National Heritage certainly, perhaps the Department for Education and Science, and the Foreign Office if work is being done with the British Council.

The system represents the classic result of a 'top down' reorganization; administrators at the bottom of the pyramid face an ever broader spread of bureaucratic systems. The local arts administrator must now deal with two or more departments of British local government, the Regional Arts Board, the Regional BFI Centre, the Area Museum Council, the region's television and broadcasting companies, the local library service and with the Regional Tourist Board. To all of these must be added the numerous quangos, foundations and trusts which will play a part in the arts administrator's work and, for many, one of the National Lottery agencies. It is hard not to lose identity and purpose in such a maze.

5.3 INDIRECT GOVERNMENT SUPPORT

The picture we have given so far, despite its apparent complexity, may still give a misleadingly simple picture of the true nature of government support for the arts in Britain. A number of important neo-governmental arts support organizations still fall outside the Ministry – the British Council, for example, which is responsible for promoting British art overseas, is funded by the Foreign Office – and there are other important sources of government grant aid and support which must be mentioned. The two most important of these are the state media (the BBC) and the state education service. (There are several others, such as the British armed forces, whose support of military bands was for many years larger than the Arts Council's total budget for music.)

There is no doubt that in the 1940s the BBC effectively acted as British government patron of the arts. As Hewison (1977) wrote:

> As an employer and promoter the BBC covered the whole field of artistic activity, directly commissioning music and plays, employing actors, writers and musicians, publishing *The Listener*, and with talks and poetry readings providing the freelance work which is an essential part of the humus needed by cultural life in order to thrive.

The BBC is generally credited with raising the taste of its wartime listeners in music; between 1942 and 1944 the proportion of 'serious' music played over the air on records rose from 6% to 40%. Yet its role as patron of writers and composers is less readily recognized. It employed among others George Orwell, Dylan Thomas and Geoffrey Grigson, and premiered musical works by among others Lennox Berkeley, Elizabeth Lutyens, Michael Tippett and Benjamin Britten. In later decades its patronage was less obvious, though even now, when many of its programmes are made by independent production companies, the BBC remains arguably the largest single employer of musicians and actors in Britain.

Less tangible, but equally important, is the value which the media gives in its programming to artists and to art. Does it divide 'serious' programmes from 'entertainment' and perpetuate the idea that one person cannot be interested in both? Does it nevertheless have good arts performances, and good exposition of art matters? Even if it does, do its most popular programmes, its soap operas for example, imply that artists and art are nothing to do with 'ordinary' lives, and so marginalize even those good arts programmes?

The taught curriculum within the state education system will have a profound effect upon people's readiness to listen to good music, look at fine art works and enjoy great drama. The arts administrator will regard schools and colleges as his natural allies in the preparation of audiences and the development of public taste. Where the state system employs drama teachers, art and music teachers, musical instrument teachers, teachers of dance and crafts specialists, these must be seen, not just as an essential part of the education service, but also as part of an overall pattern of state support for the arts. Equally, when the curriculum is redrawn to exclude arts activities, or when new financial constraints prevent school staff from taking their charges on gallery visits or to concerts and plays it must be seen as evidence of state indifference or hostility to the arts.

Equally important is the area of training of artists, administrators and those many other people who want to work in arts organizations. The most vibrant of national cultures will disintegrate unless high quality centres for research and training are maintained, and in Britain the crumbling of the once admired network of music, drama and art colleges is greatly to be deplored. There is evidence that even in those institutions which still survive, the virtually complete withdrawal of the mandatory grant system has meant that some of the students who can afford the fees are less than the best.

At a lower level, Britain is following the rest of Europe in the establishment of National Vocational Qualifications (NVQs) which give qualifications in areas such as theatre house management, and club doorkeeping. By the end of 1993 there were about 400 NVQs available across a range of occupations. (There are also broader-based General National Vocational Qualifications (GNVQs) usually available only in post-16 colleges.) This kind of training is to be welcomed as it provides a measure of ability for people seeking work in technical and service positions in arts organizations, but it will be wasted if the training for directors, artists and arts administrators (who give the organization its purpose and direction) is disintegrating at the same time.

5.4 GOVERNMENT RESTRAINTS: FINANCIAL

Two aspects of the relationship between taxation and state financial 'support' have already been mentioned. First, many taxes (but taxes on the sales of a product in particular) tend to have a doubly harmful effect on the arts: they increase production costs and take away some part of the public's leisure spending capacity. Second, there is an irritating circularity in the way in which the total tax bill (personal government taxation and local taxes) of an arts organization will sometimes be seen to amount to much the same as the grant aid returned to them by government. It is then that the arts administration begins to suspect that the system is designed to give the authorities a degree of control over the arts organization which they would not otherwise enjoy.

Governments have the means of affecting the organization in other ways. Withdrawal of funding for one of the support systems of an arts organization has a powerful effect. Cutting a local transport subsidy on key local routes, for instance, or withdrawing a travel or a parking concession can have a noticeable impact on an arts venue. National governments may adopt legislation designed to curb fraudulent selling by telephone, but it may, by putting an end to booking theatre and concert seats by telephone, do great harm to larger-scale arts organizations. Or, to take a very different example, local government may undermine the economy of a local arts organization by suddenly increasing charges for their use of meeting rooms in a local authority library or school or by introducing charges for using the local authority's advertising boards for publicity.

Often, such damage is unwittingly done by one government department acting without fully realizing the likely effects upon another. It is therefore incumbent upon the arts administrator, in addition to all other duties, to make sure that the workings of the arts organization are explained fully and at length to every interested party, including all local government departments, so that they cannot legislate, as so often, in ignorance of the likely effects.

5.5 GOVERNMENT RESTRAINTS: LICENSING

Licensing of public exhibitions and performances varies from country to country but in Britain almost every arts event requires several kinds of licence, and often requires assent to standard forms of contractual agreement between agents and managers or with the creator or performer. These involve quite intricate matters of insurance and liability, which we also touch on.

All public arts events, from open air concerts to a play in a marquee or an exhibition in a village hall, must be properly licensed. All buildings and places in which public arts events are held (including open air sites, churches and private residences) must be licensed in compliance with the numerous safety requirements set out in *Building Regulations Act 1976*. (The Home Office publishes guidelines for such matters as foyer circulation space, the space between rows of auditorium seats, emergency lighting and public signs.) All buildings and spaces used for public events must have been inspected by the Fire Authority to ensure that they meet the requirements set out in the *Fire Precautions Act 1971*. (The Home Office publishes guidance on the numerous and detailed regulations contained in this Act.)

Further, it is necessary to ensure that all parts of the venue, including those which the public does not enter, fully conform with the *Health and Safety at Work Act 1974*. This act lays down a number of obligations on employers, to provide a working environment which is safe, without health risks and adequate for employees' welfare. All employers are obliged to have a clearly written policy on these matters, to bring it clearly to the notice of employees (and to the visiting public) and to consult with safety representatives from a recognized union. If required to do so by two such representatives the employer must set up a safety committee. The employer is further required by law to report accidents involving serious injury and any dangerous incidents (such as the collapse of scaffolding or lifts, short circuits which stop work, and uncontrolled release of dangerous substances).

There is an inspectorate of the Health and Safety at Work Commission and Executive which has power to enter and inspect licensed premises, and with powers that are enforced by criminal sanctions. They will pay close attention, among other things, to hygiene: all kitchens, and vans bearing prepared food, must be inspected and licensed; all staff in them must wear the proper headgear and clothing. They will also inspect: loading and unloading conditions in store-rooms; all overhead constructions; toilets; heating and lighting in offices; and general ventilation. (The Executive has published a booklet (1994) giving detailed guidance to employers.)

When the venue has been inspected and approved as a public building, proper precautions against fire having been taken, and the health and safety of visitors having been assured, then the building may generally be used for the purposes of housing an art exhibition, or holding a public dance. (Even so it is wise to make certain that no local by-laws are being contravened; for example, in some areas public events may not be held late at night.)

A further step is necessary to license a play, opera, ballet, pantomime or any other kind of dramatic performance. The administrator must hold a theatre licence in compliance with Sections 12–20 and the First Schedule of the *Theatres Act 1968*. These licences are usually awarded annually (although it is possible to have an occasional licence when the venue is not going to be much used during the year). Application is made to the local district council, who will, before issuing the licence, require statements from the relevant officers that the three acts mentioned above have been complied with. (It is worth noting that a drama performance is still a public performance even if no payment is made for admission; a 'happening' staged in a street will thus require a public licence.)

If films are to be shown on more than six days in the year then application must be made for a cinema licence under the terms of the *Cinematograph Acts 1909* and *1952*. The building or structure used must conform to the building regulations, fire regulations and health and safety regulations outlined above. If it is a moving structure, such as in a travelling exhibition, the administrator may take out a licence from his normal address which can be used throughout the tour, but he must then give two days notice to the licensing authority and the chief of police of each area in which the show is going to take place.

There are two other important points to be made about the cinema licence. First, the 1952 Act defines cinematograph exhibitions as being 'an exhibition of moving pictures produced on a screen by means which include the projection of light'. It would therefore seem that video, closed circuit relays and the showing of television programmes in public places do not require this licence. Second,

Section 5 exempts two types of film show from the need to have a cinema licence – wholly private (i.e. domestic) film exhibitions and those to which anyone is admitted without payment.

Behind these exemptions is a wish to leave organizations free to use films either for specialist or for general educational purposes. People who try to use these exemptions for other ends, running a private 'adult' cinema club, for example, should know that Section 4 of the 1909 Act gives the licensing authorities and the police the right to enter all premises known to be, or suspected of, showing films, whether licensed or not, and that the general law governing obscenity covers private exhibitions as fully as public ones. If the licensing authorities find anything amiss on a visit they may serve either an improvement notice requiring faults to be remedied within a specified period, or, if the faults are in serious contravention of the law they may serve a prohibition notice, which means the immediate closure of the premises.

The arts administrator who manages premises has, in addition to insuring art works, performers and staff, the duty to insure the premises and the public which lawfully visits them. As it is customary for an arts venue to be owned by a company or local government authority which is quite separate from the management operating the building, it is important to be clear about their separate responsibilities. Each has 'a common duty of care'. Under the *Occupiers' Liability Act 1957* the owners of a building have a duty to make sure the building is safe before it is let to any management. The management which rents the building has a duty to maintain the building, to make certain that all the requirements of fire precaution, and health and safety at work are fully complied with, and to make certain that building, artworks, artists, staff and public are properly insured (it may be that the building's owners pay some of the insurance premiums, but it is nevertheless the operating management which must make certain it is done).

Claims can of course be made against the arts venue management for a variety of reasons, ranging from personal injury sustained on the premises to clothing being damaged. (Bertram Mills' circus once had to pay damages to virtually every member of a large audience when it was discovered that the newly painted seats had not properly dried.) If it is suggested that the building itself was defective – say, for example, someone has fallen through a stair tread – then the building's owners will be liable for damages. If it is something which a daily inspection should have noticed and corrected, someone tripping over a loose stair rod, for example, then the management will be held responsible. It should be noted that the 'common duty of care' extends beyond compliance with regulations. Owners and occupiers are expected by the law (and the insurance companies) to foresee unusual difficulties and to guard against them. As Arnold-Baker (1983) notes: 'That is why a guard dog can be a mixed blessing: he does not always appreciate the legal difference between a lawful visit and a trespass.'

In addition to the licensing of the building and being licensed to present stage or cinema shows in it, the arts administrator must also hold the necessary licences to run restaurants and bars within the venue (we elaborate on this in the following chapter). Also, a fact which often surprises newcomers to arts administration, the arts administrator is responsible for seeing that the necessary royalty on all plays and operas performed under his or her administration is promptly paid (and a licence to perform obtained) and that permission is given (and payment made, when necessary) for the reproduction of pictures, photographs, poems, book extracts or diagrams that are displayed in the programme or in advertising matter. Royalties on all music, whether recorded or 'live', in all kinds of venue must be paid to the Performing Rights Society who will require a weekly account of the music played. Further, royalties must also be paid to the Authors' Licensing and Collecting Society for any copyright work duplicated for use within the organization.

In all, the arts administrator will note that the same government authorities which 'support' the arts, also impel them to conform to a complex framework of government legislation. Once, Dionysus stood on common land and played his lute to attract the crowds to his riotous entertainments. Now he would have to spend many hours making applications to various officials to license his pitch and his show, and then making returns to the authorities who would quickly demand taxes, fees and royalties from him.

REFERENCES

Arnold-Baker, C. (1983) *Practical Law for Arts Administrators.*
Baumol, W.J. and Baumol, H. (1985) 'The future of the theatre and the cost disease of the arts', in *Bach and the Box* (1985).
Baumol, W.J. and Bowen, W.G. (1966) *Performing Arts: the Economic Dilemma.*
CIPFA Leisure and Recreation Statistics, 1992/3.
Department of National Heritage Annual Report 1994.
Harrod, R. (1951) *The Life of John Maynard Keynes.*
Hewison, R. (1977) *Under Siege.*
Peacock, A. (1993) *Paying the Piper: Culture, Music and Money.*
Peacock, A., Shoesmith, E. and Milner G. (1983) *Cost Inflation in the Performed Arts.*
Titmuss, R. (1970) *Commitment to Welfare.*
Titmuss, R. (1974) *Social Policy.*
Wilson Knight, G. (1962) *The Golden Labyrinth.*

Arts programming

6.1 FUNDING THE PROGRAMME

The visual arts in Britain are substantially supported by state aid. However, the literary and performing arts are largely supported by the paying public. The accounts of many theatres and concert halls, most cinemas, clubs and conference centres, and all publishers will show that their income does not come primarily from the state but from members of the public who pay to enjoy their works.

Nevertheless, there are few arts organizations which are not at some point circumscribed by the state, if only because licensing and taxation involve private commercial organizations as much as public ones. And all arts organizations are as one in that among the first administrative decisions that have to be made is how the proper audience for each piece of work may be fully realized. That necessarily involves performing arts organizations drawing up budgets which pose the question: will we be able to reach our necessary income targets simply by selling, at the right price, to the proper audience? For gallery administrators the question may be rather different, but they have also to ask how they can draw in the best possible public to view and benefit from the art on display.

The 'proper' audience, for any art, is of course difficult to define. It might be thought to include all those people from the possible catchment area who might draw pleasure and benefit from the work, including people of all ages, from all ethnic minorities and disadvantaged groups, and with quite different income levels. But even such a noble definition does not in practice take us very far. Ethnic minorities have quirky interests like all other groups, and are not always best served by a patronizing service of what liberal bureaucrats think is 'their' culture. Low wage earners may get more pleasure and benefit from a familiar 'good night out' than a heavily subsidized seat at the opera. So may high wage earners. Conversely we may find that an operatic aria (used perhaps to advertise a sporting event) suddenly becomes hugely popular and draws large audiences to concert halls. Administrators must constantly learn from experience (their own and others') about the likely audience, must constantly seek to widen their experience by redressing apparently unwarranted imbalances in the composition of that audience, and must hope, and expect, to be surprised. To these matters, and the linked question of pricing, we return below in Chapters 7 and 8.

For some of the larger entertainment corporations, and for a fair proportion of the amateur arts, the following questions of funding do not apply. Equally, for those museums and galleries that are overwhelmingly funded by government, and have no regular admission charge, only one or two of the following categories have direct relevance. For a large number of arts organizations, however, income is compounded of 'box office', grant aid from governmental and neo-governmental sources, grant aid from other trusts and foundations, commercial sponsorship, merchandising, regular fundraising schemes and special fundraising drives.

Although there is much publicity given to the last four items, arts organizations still get most of their income from the general public's attendance, next most from national and local government sources, a little from commercial sponsorship and (for the most part) only a minuscule part from other activities. Some British arts administrators point out that in low-profile areas of the arts the time and effort expended on trying to gain commercial sponsorship shows a net loss, and that having to show government funding agencies that efforts have been made to gain funding from every possible commercial source is more a political gesture than a realistic economic strategy.

Thus, the accounts of a medium-scale civic theatre in Britain will show that although in numerical terms its support from its local authority has remained constant, grant-aiding of, say, £350 000 a year, which ten years ago was 50% of total budget, is now less than 20% of an annual turnover which will probably now exceed £2 000 000. The revenue grants from other trusts and foundations, commercial sponsorship, merchandising and fund raising efforts will usually total 5% of turnover or less. There are plenty of examples of good fund raising schemes: for example, the Friends of the reopened Blackpool Grand Theatre contributed £70 000 a year to funds.

The following figures (Table 6.1) give a broad picture of income sources within one sector of the arts economy, Arts Council clients.

Within the crafts area, which in terms of economic structure lies midway between the heavily subsidized galleries and commercial entertainment, the immediate reliance on grant aid is roughly comparable, at between 35% and 40%. Figures for the Crafts Council show this clearly, though public funding is proportionately very much lower in the wider realms of crafts work, large parts of which are wholly commercial, and would not be included in the Crafts Council's published figures. (See Table 6.2.)

Thus an arts administrator needs, within the chosen area of work, to be realistic both about the ability of the 'proper' audience to pay, and about any supplementary contribution likely to be made by various funding sources. He or she needs, in a word, to be skilled in the political *realpolitik* of grant application.

Table 6.1 Income sources of Arts Council clients

Income sources (£ million)	1991/2 actual	1992/3 estimated	1993/4 estimated
Earned	136	137	131
Sponsorship	24	26	27
ACGB	111	113	113
Local authorities and			
other public bodies	27	26	26
Total	298	302	297
Attendances (million)	11.80	11.69	11.78
Income ratios (%)			
Self-generated	54	54	56
ACGB	37	37	38
Local authorities and			
other public bodies	8	9	9

Table 6.2 Sales and income of the Crafts Council

Crafts Council (£ thousands)	1991/2	1992/3	1993/4
Income from fund raising and sponsorship	30	46	65
Income from exhibitions in gallery and on tour	27	104	27
Direct sales	798	1116	1005
Sales generated by Crafts Council events	3000	4600	5000
Total public funding	2820	2980	3350

We have now reached the central territory of much modern arts administration, and an area in which the battle between the arts administrator and the planning bureaucrat is at its fiercest. In repeating the general guidelines for good grant application, it must be borne in mind that it is the arts bureaucracy that creates guidelines for applicants, and the arts bureaucracy which assesses them. The danger is therefore that making a successful grant application may compromise some crucial element in the arts organization's activities and beliefs, may involve yielding to the bureaucrats' wish to standardize cultural 'services', and as a result may put the vibrant holistic management of an organization in thrall to an external agency.

With these warnings in mind however, it is possible to list general guidelines for good applications. For people unused to the arts world, for whom making a grant application may be just a matter of writing to a local trust, the detailed and sophisticated procedures which must be followed are quite a surprise.

Any applicant, whether for a capital project, project funding or for revenue funding, must usually assemble at least the following:

- Detailed and realistic costings of the project (together with all longer-term cost implications) must be worked out.
- The proportion of costs or necessary annual income that can reasonably be borne by supporters and by the general public needs to be realistically assessed.
- When this is done, create a business plan which gives outlines of all expenditure and (realistic) income for the next 3–4 years.
- Thoroughly research the purposes and functions of all funding bodies, public and private, that might be interested in your work, and organize your activities so that you can immediately present your case to them in a sustained and positive way.
- Create a realistic merchandising and fund raising strategy which complements your major activities.

Nowadays a sophisticated business plan will have written into it 'best case' and 'worst case' scenarios, and will be subject to regular modification. The paperwork (and office time) involved is considerable. The bodies to which you make application will all need copies of your business plans, anticipated layouts, programming strategies, minutes of public meetings, 'mission statements' and other public declarations. Increasingly, applicants are also required to have had a feasibility study carried out by an approved external agency.

Government support

The first step towards gaining government or local government support is thoroughly to research the requirements of the many grant-aiding schemes operated by the four arts councils, regional arts boards, British Film Institute, Crafts Council, Museums and Galleries Commission and of course the local authority councils which cover the area in which the group or organization works. The great majority of arts grants go to properly constituted organizations concerned primarily with promoting excellence or fostering innovation in art, which have charitable status, a properly constituted board representative of most of the largest and most significant groups in the community, which are well and openly managed, responsive to public comment, and which are willing that all their activities be subject to scrutiny and assessment.

Government support means regular government scrutiny, and for some that is an intolerable intrusion. As the founder of Portable Theatre said in 1971:

> We were doing everything and it gave the show a lot of life because it was inspired by very few people, but you hit a growth point where you either let yourself become an organization or you say no, we're not going to become involved in anything like that. Now its got an £8000 subsidy from the Arts Council and its like some monster. We don't want anything to do with it any longer because it'll shape us rather than let us shape it. You have to report to the Arts Council and announce what your future plans are. Who wants to do that?

David Hare's outburst might seem 'sad', as the then finance director of the Arts Council commented (Field, 1973), but this is something about which artists and artists' groups feel strongly. Applying for, and gaining, state support inevitably involves full cooperation with government bureaucracies which, however sensitive, will do something to congeal the normative spirit of the group, and will lessen the sense of adventure that young arts ventures always have.

There could have been other ways of doing things, of course. Speaking of the Arts Council's treatment of Joan Littlewood, of which she herself has complained (Littlewood, 1994), Field went on to say:

> Perhaps it would have been better to have offered her substantial amounts, say £50 000 per annum for three years only, and sent her away to 'do her thing'. All her best work would have been done and she would have moved to something different, instead of dissipating her energies on attempting to raise funds, and diluting her artistic talents in making compromises to meet West End requirements.

But the government support systems in Britain have become less flexible, not more, and are becoming increasingly rigid. The notion that an artist might one day be given a huge sum of public money and be told, in Somerset Maugham's unlovely phrase, 'to go to hell and back' is less and less likely. Economic accountability is generally held to be more important than artistic accountability. This rigidity is a result in part of the proliferation of matching grant schemes, and also because funders increasingly guard against 'double funding' by fully acquainting themselves with all details of an arts organization's other income. The 'tie-in' between the Department of National Heritage and private business sponsorship through the Business Sponsorship Incentive Scheme is for example one of the growth areas in arts funding (Table 6.3).

Table 6.3 Government grant-aided and commercial sponsorship

£ millions	1991/2 actual	1992/3 actual	1993/4 estimate
DNH grant	3.5	4.4	4.5
Sponsorship attracted from first-time sponsors	4.6	4.5	4.5
Total sponsorship attracted	6.3	7.5	7.5

The figures show how close is the link between public and private money.

Other sources: trusts and foundations

The arts administrator must be fully acquainted with international and national trusts and foundations that may be interested in funding his work. Nor is it wise to neglect local sources – it is estimated that in Britain more than three billion pounds is lying untouched in neglected charitable bequests. (Under the terms of the *Charities Act 1992* a bank or building society is allowed to inform the commissioners if it holds a charity account which has not been used for five years or more; if it finds it is no longer being administered the charity commissioners may direct the bank or building society to pay the idle sum into the account of another local charity with similar purposes.)

The major international sources of funding for British arts administrators are the many and varied European funds available. We have already discussed the significant contribution made to renovation and development of arts buildings in Britain by the European Development Fund. There are many other European funds open to application for those seeking revenue for programming. These, itemized for British arts administrators by the European Forum for Arts and Heritage in Brussels, include the funds of the Commission for Culture (in 1993/4 about £10 million) and schemes such as the Kaleidoscope scheme to 'encourage cross-border artistic effort' (about £2.2 million). One may expect British government and European schemes to become more closely integrated in the coming years, although some international sources of funding, such as the Gulbenkian Foundation, will remain largely outside the bureaucratic net.

For a trawl through the national trusts and foundations likely to offer help, the arts administrator will need to be equipped with the annual *Directory of Grant Making Trusts*, published by the Directory of Social Change. This shows the parameters of each trust's interests and offers examples of organizations recently helped. Since its creation in 1991 the most significant national body in this field has been the Foundation for Sport and the Arts, which out of its annual income of £60 million (from donations from the Pools Promoters' Association) gives around £20 million to the arts. It is reluctant to give grants which go towards the payment of wages, but prefers grant-aiding particular project developments by smaller and newer organizations. In 1993 it introduced a maximum grant limit of £150 000. It processes grants more rapidly than most other funding organizations, dealing with some 500 applications per week, and giving answers in less than three months.

The requirements of an application to the Foundation for Sport and the Arts offer useful guidelines for applicants to any trust or foundation. They require:

1. background details of and the general purposes of the organization making the application;
2. up-to-date financial statements;
3. clear description of the purposes for which grant is sought (including reports from professional consultants);
4. a budget detailing costs of the project, the amount asked for from the organization, and full details of sought or committed money from other sources;
5. information about all those involved in the realization of the project (suppliers, contractors, etc.);
6. details of the legal status of the applicant organization;
7. how many people, and from which parts of the community, will benefit from the proposed scheme;
8. any significant expressions of support from noteworthy sources.

(The Foundation also requires a separate summary of the proposal set out on a single sheet of A4 paper and the completion of a questionnaire which it will send to applicants.)

It is not clear whether the reordering of spending that follows the introduction of Britain's new National Lottery in 1994 will finally affect the Foundation for Sport and the Arts. Early estimates suggested that the new lottery, created by the *National Lottery Act 1993*, was expected to have an annual turnover of at least £2 billion so the effects on the Foundation, and on charity-giving generally, were likely to be considerable. It was further expected that the proportionate share of the lottery proceeds to be distributed amongst applicants by the four UK arts councils would be between £100 and £200 million. These, it was expected, would go largely, but not exclusively, on capital projects.

There are two intangibles in this. The first is that nobody can ever forecast with much precision what effect such a huge new factor will have on existing patterns of leisure spending. The two billion and more spent on the new national lottery is not new money, and there will be an effect, albeit hard to define precisely, on spending at the box office of concert halls and theatres, on buying records and books and on the holiday business. The government will not forego tax (the rate of Lottery Duty was set immediately at 12%) but some arts administrators may well find that they lose out to the lottery: the televised 'grand draw' will affect their box offices directly, and the change in leisure spending patterns will affect them indirectly. The money 'returned' to the arts will be returned to some arts organizations in the form of capital funding, but it may be taken from the box office revenue of them all.

The second intangible is the likely falling away in support. Over time, non-winners, who are the overwhelming majority, become disillusioned and spend their money on other things. (There may too be incidents which bring more rapid disillusionment, as when the kidnap and murder of the son of a winner of the Sydney Opera Lottery, effectively ended public interest in it.) Certainly, the lotteries run by local government, set up under the *Lotteries and Amusements Act 1976*, started well. Three years after the act there were 5 000 lotteries being held annually in Britain, with income exceeding £32 million. But ten years after the act the total income had dwindled to an annual £5 million, little more than 1% of the £486 million Britons were then spending on the pools. So it is wise to remember that spending within the area of gambling is relatively volatile, and that although administrators may be much occupied, at present, by lottery applications, this will not necessarily be a permanent state.

Commercial sponsorship

Like other areas of funding, commercial sponsorship is becoming increasingly enmeshed within the state support system. Formerly, when it was a much larger proportion of arts funding than now, it operated quite independently, and gaining support for the building of a new concert hall or gallery was a matter of local initiative by a group of businessmen, or, quite often, simple philanthropy by a successful local industrialist.

Swingeing post-war taxation supposedly killed off private patronage. People like John Christie of Glyndebourne; Barry Jackson of the Birmingham Rep and Malvern; and Samuel Courtauld, prime benefactor of the Courtauld Institute of Art, could no longer, under the new taxation, afford to be generous. So, although such acts of philanthropy still happily occur (Billy Butlin, Rocco Forte, and Richard Branson among others, have, in their different ways, offered private support since then to the arts in Britain) most commercial support of the arts is now corporate sponsorship given through official schemes. At the centre of these, working in close conjunction with the four British arts councils, is ABSA, the Association for Business Sponsorship of the Arts.

ABSA was formed in 1976, with the aid of a small government grant, by the joining together of six leading business houses who each put in £1000. By 1979 it was spending some £1.5 million on the arts out of a total estimated commercial sponsorship of £3 million. By 1993/4 total commercial sponsorship was estimated to be running in the region of £60 million.

It is important to stress that ABSA sees its role largely as a broker, encouraging sponsorship and then putting commercial organizations in touch with arts ventures. It has an increasing skills-sharing role, particularly through its Business in the Arts scheme, which encourages people in business to share their management skills with the arts. Its function is also to create the climate in which arts administrators can approach possible industrial sponsors for themselves. The advice to such administrators is always to:

- clearly determine which part of your enterprise requires help;
- carefully research local commerce to discover which local commercial organization(s) might be interested;
- in the application say how much is needed, what difference the sponsorship will make and who will benefit;
- detail clearly and unromantically what advantages the sponsorship will bring to the donor.

When a happy match is made, the sponsor may not need much encouragement to do it again, as the advantages will be obvious. However, all sponsors need 'nursing'. They must be invited to events so that they can see for themselves the benefits to the community they have helped to foster. They must be sent reports of successes, video films of events they miss, copies of letters of thanks. In return the arts organization will expect to hear of ways in which association with an arts venue seems to be benefiting the sponsor.

Merchandising, and foyer sales

The gallery shop, the foyer postcard stand, tapes and compact discs, museum sales catalogue, and the arts centre bookshop may not only provide useful income, but are part of an impression which forms in the public mind of a lively and interesting organization. Many visitors, and particularly tourists, feel cheated if they cannot buy some significant memento of the fact that they have enjoyed being in an arts venue, however brief their visit may have been. In many venues, having many other attractions set around the ticket sales counter also gives a fillip to advance bookings by the locals.

Most important is the income generated by bars, restaurants and coffee shops. Even in quite small venues it is not unusual to find that a third of total income is from bar sales and refreshments, while some larger arts organizations with considerable foyer space find that their catering turnover in a year exceeds £1 million. Again, such amenities are not simply profitable, they also contribute greatly to the ambience of the venue, encourage people to arrive early and stay late (and thus spend more within the venue itself) and boost advance ticket sales, particularly if the ticket counter is open after the show as well as before it.

Some venues franchise their catering, which means that all the responsibilities of kitchen hygiene, stock keeping, portion control and service are taken from them, and in addition they receive a (usually quite modest) fee from the catering company. However, in some instances administrators have found that they have also relinquished quality control as well, and that the caterer is inflexible to suggestions such as 'themed' food to accompany one item in the programme, or to the needs of special receptions. When parts of the franchised service – keeping the bars open after performances, or opening coffee bars for early morning shoppers – seem to be unprofitable, they tend to be discontinued, and the administrator may then find he or she has too little control, and may regret the franchising arrangement.

The best results seem to derive from the foyer services (restaurants, bars and shops) being run by a separate trading company which is legally distinct from the management company, but managed by its appointees. Assistants may be drawn from the 'friends' of the arts organization, but experience suggests that such service should, even if unpaid, be given by people who have been trained for the task and who submit to professional discipline. The paid management, on behalf of the trading company, will take responsibility for applying to the Justices for any necessary bar licence. (Although under the *Theatres Act 1968* no ordinary on-licence is required if a full theatre licence has been obtained, an application must usually be lodged in any case for a restaurant on-licence, and it is courteous to give notice of intention to the Justices so that any general objections about the overall operation may be heard.) The catering or foyer services manager will also take responsibility for compliance with the *Health and Safety at Work Act 1974*. Under this arrangement the venue management and foyer management can act in harmony, but without the day-to-day problems of catering and arts activities being borne by one person.

Fund raising

Fund raising has become a specialist department in some arts organizations, and there are many conferences and publications purporting to teach this specialism to others. (These are always rather expensive, and often prompt the thought that anybody capable of paying the large fees involved hardly needs instruction in fund raising.) There are also professional fund raisers, who may be hired by arts organizations to raise funds for particular projects. These have certainly notched up successes, although there have also been some spectacular failures, and it remains true that for most organizations fund raising still yields a small part of total income.

There are several government-inspired schemes which can yield regular funds to an arts organization. The first is the well-tried system of covenanting money to an arts organization. Covenants are undertaken for a minimum of four years, and offer the recipient a bonus in the form of reclaimed 'tax'. A second system is payroll giving. From 1987 people who are at work and paying PAYE have been able to give up to £120 a year to a charitable arts organization as a deduction from their pay and obtain tax relief on it.

Many other schemes exist by which supporters of a particular arts project can give to funds. There are the programmes of events run by friends and helpers – coffee mornings, mock auctions, raffles, garden parties, fêtes, lunches, discos – which can be profitable but which can also take up a disproportionate amount of time and effort for very little reward, and can diffuse the organizational aim. (There is a familiar story of some worthies raising funds to reopen their local theatre who cannot think what they will do with their evenings once it is open again.) There are also sad stories of big losses being made by fund raisers on badly-advertised charity concerts, badly-run lotteries and on outdoor galas where the weather ruined an uninsured event.

It is probably safer not to pitch expectations from such events too high, and to rely on safer routines such as public collections or the promotion of an affinity card. This is a credit card bearing the name of the arts organization for which the bank pays a sum of money to the organization for each person taking one out, and thereafter pays a modest 'interest' to the named organization on each transaction.

6.2 WHICH ARTISTS AND WHICH ART?

In each art form there are a few artists who have been made rich by their work, rather more who consistently make a living, and many more than that whose income from their art work is not enough to sustain them. In part this is the result of chance, in part a reflection of quantity and quality, and in part it is a reflection of the unpredictable currents of popular taste. It is also the result of critical decisions made by arts bureaucrats and by arts administrators about which work is to be placed before the public, and in what context.

Almost always the arts administrator's choice is limited by what is available. In the same way an agent may wish that the world's best instrumental players were clients, but if all of today's best players are already represented, then the agent must represent others and hope that a young performer on the books will turn out to be one of tomorrow's acknowledged greats. Similarly, a cinema manager may wish for a blockbuster every week, but has to be contented sometimes with what is on release and available on that date. A gallery director may wish for a compelling new exhibition every month, but has to choose between those artists who are not already showing nor preparing for a show elsewhere, who have work available, and would like to be shown in that gallery.

Not infrequently, arts administrators will bemoan their lack of choice. 'I can only put on what's available' is a familiar grumble of the medium-sized non-producing theatre manager, who knows that there are far fewer shows 'on the road' than there were fifteen years ago, and that among them the quality shows which will fill the auditorium are both expensive and difficult to book. A large city venue can be asked to pay a weekly guarantee of more than £100 000 to a big touring musical, which has to play for at least three weeks for the hiring management to break even, or they find they can only book big name acts for one or two nights, and have to charge £30 (and more) a ticket to recoup the artistes' fees. A smaller venue will find that it cannot afford either, that its stage facilities are not adequate for a top-line show, and that its more limited seating would in any case mean that the ticket prices would have to be ridiculously inflated.

The administrator then faces another problem. Some of the shows and performers that can be presented by the venue are not well known. The administrator is thus asked to book shows, exhibitions and even films 'sight unseen'. The problem is sometimes exacerbated by the fact that a funding body has already, in part, funded a 'tour' of this work, and so the administrator is under some pressure to book in work which others know and approve of, but which may not be right for this particular theatre, gallery or concert hall.

The problem would be far less acute if there were just a few high quality critics in each art form on whose judgement the administrator could rely. But there are too many critical pulpits, and of too variable a quality. Every advertising sheet for every artist and every show contains carefully presented commendations, but the news that the *Northern Courier* has said that the show is 'one on its own', or that the *Eastern Gazette* has pronounced an artist 'one of the distinctive voices in the twentieth century madhouse' is of little help to the administrator. Even quotations from known and usually reliable sources are sometimes presented out of context, and in a misleading highly-edited form.

The administrator of the large urban venue has by contrast not only got the uncut reviews of known critics, on radio or in the national press, but has the box office returns from similar venues with whom he or she is in close professional contact. The administrator of a rural arts centre has none of these advantages. Between the two are many administrators who are from time to time disadvantaged by having to make choices about their programme on less than full personal knowledge of the work available. In all, except in the large national and regional venues, 'booking blind' can be a problem.

There are therefore three important steps that must be taken:

- The administrator must bring the fullest possible previously-acquired knowledge of relevant art and artists to the work: there are always limitations to what may be learned 'on the job'.
- The administrator must build up a network of reliable and friendly contacts: artists, sympathetic members of the public, fellow administrators, whose critical judgement can be relied upon.
- There must be regular opportunity for the arts administrator to attend arts activities outside his or her administration, so that there is a constantly refreshed sense of what it is like to be a member of an audience or of an arts workshop, or to be working as an artist or performer. Sometimes, to quote from the first edition of *Arts Administration* (1980), the administrator is too ready to become 'rather like the man with the key to the pearly gates; he is continually passing people through but never gets the chance to enjoy the other side'.

6.3 PROGRAMMING

For some arts administrators questions of selecting and balancing a programme do not arise. Sir Stephen Waley-Cohen, for example, does not have to consider what to present on the stage of London's St Martin's Theatre each evening: so far as anyone can foresee, it will be Agatha Christie's *The Mousetrap*. Most administrators are, however, faced with making a series of choices. They have to select work for which they think a 'proper' audience can be found. They have to decide how frequently, or for what length of time, it can be shown, how it fits into an overall programme and, usually, what kinds of prices should be charged for admission. For each venue the solutions to these questions will be different. So, we can only offer a few general comments here, rather than final answers.

When building up a mixed programme, it is wise to think of the potential audience not as one mass, but as a series of interlinked units. A very small 'core' audience at an arts centre may come to all kinds of event (film-making classes, dance presentations, gallery shows, jazz concerts, plays and lectures) but most people will come regularly only to one or two kinds of event, and others will only come to one. Experience suggests that half of the people attending jazz concerts in an arts centre will only come for jazz events, while less than 10% of them go to everything else in the centre's programme.

So, the audience for each separate strand in the programme needs to be considered separately. How often do the jazz attenders want concerts? May that dedicated audience be gradually enlarged by having, say, weekly instead of fortnightly jazz sessions? Or would that mean that the same number of people would choose to come less frequently, effectively cutting the average attendance? In general, the arts administrator will find there is a rhythm to the programme which suits the various audience units. The film audience may happily come twice a week, whereas the chamber music audience may be happiest with a monthly recital. An exhibition may outstay its welcome in four weeks, but there may be complaints if it hangs only for ten days. Excepting festivals, for which a special audience is recruited, the administrator must avoid 'bunching up' a programme so that there is too much of one art form, or genre, presented in a short period. That will both infuriate followers of other kinds of event ('Five weeks of films and no dance!'), and make supporters of the favoured art form angry because they cannot afford either the time or the extra cash the programme suddenly demands from them.

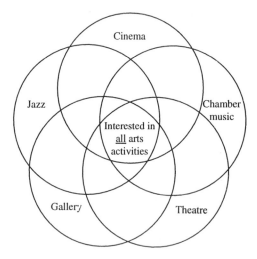

Figure 3 The overlapping audience

There are similar problems over the regularity with which a particular artist's work is exposed. The administrator needs to balance the need to 'nurse' a growing audience with regular shows, with the fact that the audience may not want to see an artist's work again after too short an interval. As ever, particular judgement is called for in particular circumstances. Bernard Samuels built up Beryl Cooke's reputation by regular shows at the Plymouth Arts Centre, which drew ever-larger crowds. Conversely there have been many civic theatre managers who, encouraged by the fact that a 'one man show' has been well received, have rebooked it a few months later and have found it plays to near-empty houses. The ability to find the right 'rhythm' for artists and for particular art forms is one of the arts administrator's keenest skills.

We turn later to a discussion of pricing (Chapter 8). It is of course a vital part of the programmer's skill. At this stage we would only observe that it is a mistake to price each show within a programme simply on its cost. If one divides the cost of the show by the number of seats expected to be sold then some shows, such as touring opera, will of course be hugely expensive, and others, such as a local jazz group, will be ridiculously cheap. That simplistic pricing will have three bad effects:

- extremes in pricing may affect the numbers attracted to each event;
- neither is likely to attract its 'proper' audience, as some genuine opera lovers will not be able to afford to come, while some jazz fans may downgrade a cheaply-priced event and stay away;
- it places the activities in quite different economic and social compartments, and makes it harder to achieve the 'knock on' effect, whereby the jazz follower is tempted to try *Peter Grimes* and the opera buff encouraged to sample Chris Barber's Jazz Band.

A skilful administrator will use the enhanced profits of one cheaply-staged part of the programme to 'subsidize' another, so that the potential audience does not make its choices solely on the basis of what is affordable.

REFERENCES

Field, A. (1973) 'Disestablishing the Arts: seeking cultural alternatives', in Greyser, A. (ed) *Cultural Policy and Arts Administration* (1973).
Littlewood, J. (1994) *Joan's Book.*
The ABSA/W.H. Smith Sponsorship Manual.
The Directory of Grant Making Trusts.

Arts marketing

7.1 POTENTIAL AUDIENCES

No arts administrator will assemble a programme without considering at each stage the potential audience for the work. If the administrator does not believe that a 'proper' audience (in the sense we used the term above, p.89) can be found for each work from within that potential audience, then it is plainly unwise to programme it. As the administrator pencils in any exhibition, film or recital, he or she must have a realizable audience, preferably one 'proper' to that work, already in mind.

It is no use pretending that any amount of information, field work or particular marketing formula will ensure that the administrator's belief that there is a proper and realizable audience for a work is always justified. Even the best administrators will sometimes find their 'hunches' about the likely appeal of shows can be misplaced. The exhibition thought certain to be a great attraction may hang for a month in near-empty galleries. Conversely a marginal event, of which the administrator had no great hopes, will suddenly be a huge success. For example, the authors remember with astonishment a Polish Dance Company packing a theatre in rural Somerset. At the other end of the spectrum, in 1993 virtually every marketer and every fixer on Broadway worked on reshaping a £5.8 million musical, *Red Shoes*, to suit that well-researched market. It closed after four performances.

The arts marketing consultant Keith Diggle (1994) has neatly defined the task of marketing, and in the process has helped to define further our notion of a 'proper' audience:

The aim of arts marketing is to bring an appropriate number of people, drawn from the widest possible range of social background, economic condition and age, into an appropriate form of contact with the artist and, in so doing, to arrive at the best financial outcome that is compatible with the achievement of that aim.

To people without experience of the field it may seem that such a statement simply begs other questions: what is an 'appropriate' number of people, and an 'appropriate' form of contact? Yet, in practice, this definition proves helpful. The appropriate number of people, and the appropriate form of contact are, in a real situation, clearly indicated by the capacity of the venue, the nature and composition of the potential audience, and by the kind of work which is to be shown in it.

What this definition suggests also is that amongst other things successful marketing depends upon show and venue being properly matched. An experienced artist will usually recognize that a mismatch is being suggested. A painter may feel that the reputation and clientele of a gallery do not suit his or her work. Or the venue's size may be wrong, as when Noël Coward was urged to play a season at the vast London Palladium (Coward 1982):

> I have quite definitely decided not to do a season at the Palladium. Much as I love the theatre and the efficiency and niceness of all concerned, it's not really my ambience. I could hold them all right for a quarter of an hour or even twenty minutes but not forty five minutes. Oh no. Me for the more intimate lark to my own type of audience.

An inexperienced artist may be less fortunate, and be persuaded to show work in an unsuitable venue, giving the marketer a near-impossible task and, more importantly, blighting the artist's subsequent chances of recognition and success.

Assuming however that artist and venue are reasonably matched, what is there to be said about the potential audience? As with many things, it is easier to say what it is not. The potential audience does *not* consist only of those few people that experience suggests are bound to find the work interesting, most of whom will probably come. The kind of publicity which limply says something like: 'Those of you who enjoyed Joe Bloggs' last exhibition/concert at this venue will need no urging to come again. Joe looks forward to seeing many of his old friends. Some of the programme is new, but there will be many old favourites ....' is lazy and, human mortality being what it is, likely to yield ever-diminishing returns.

A more constructive starting point is to assume that the potential audience for each arts event comprises everyone to whom information about the event is made available, whose desire to attend can be engaged by promotion for the event and for whom the event is accessible. Those rather different concepts give us three general foundation stones in building up guidelines for arts marketing.

a) Availability of information

Information about arts events needs to be widely and readily available to all potential audiences in all possible forms throughout an extended period leading up to each event. That information (in the form of brochures, fliers, display advertisements in tourist brochures, specialist publications, and local and national newspapers, radio and television advertising, hanging cards, posters, car stickers or 'giveaways') must contain all necessary information (broad description of the genre to which the work belongs, dates, venue, hours of opening, admission prices, special amenities available, addresses and telephone numbers) and it must be accurate in every respect.

The arts administrator must spread the information about a programme as widely as possible. Is there information about local arts programmes readily available to every visitor to an area? That is, is it invariably in the ship's brochure, in-flight magazine, or taxi cab in which the potential visitor may travel? Are there posters in the train and bus station? Hotel lobby? Local bars and coffee shops? Has the local tourist information centre got full up-to-date information? Remembering that research suggests that audiences for very different leisure pursuits contain considerable crossover, is there information also available in places such as local sporting arenas, night clubs, caravan parks and restaurants? Nearer home, do all visitors to the venue itself leave with information on the coming programme? And equally importantly, is all distracting out-of-date information immediately removed from the public's attention?

Once begun, each point of information must be kept 'live'. It is positively harmful, when it has been regular practice to put a panel advertisement in a newspaper on a certain day each week, to drop it for a week or two. Even if the venue is temporarily inactive, the contact with the potential audience must be reliably maintained. For some members of the potential audience that panel is their only source of information, and even in a fallow period it may be supplying information which helps people to decide to come to later presentations, or to pass information to friends.

People vary greatly in how far ahead they plan their leisure time. Some like to book a year or more ahead for shows; others only consider booking a few days in advance; still others prefer to go 'on impulse'. Information about a programme must therefore be widely available in an accurate and up-to-date form throughout the longest possible period before the event itself.

b) Promotion

Failure to understand the distinction between simply advertising an event and promoting it leads to many sad inquests on administrative failure. 'I can't think why nobody came, we had advertisements everywhere!' Yet the plain truth is that people constantly have competing claims made upon their attention, time and money. It is estimated that in the course of a day more than 1200 products and services act upon the consciousness of those who live and work in urban Britain, and simply informing people is not enough. Only the most devoted followers of an artist's work will attend if all that is offered is information. There must be promotional work, different in kind for each artist and each art event, but strong enough to claim attention alongside the promotions of packaged holidays, convenience foods and fashionable clothing.

Promotions highlight especially attractive features of an arts event to a range of possible attenders, and they take many different forms. Sometimes an event is simply promoted by the well-written and well-illustrated material in a brochure. That material must accurately convey the nature of the entertainment. (The authors once promoted the delightful film *Closely Observed Trains* so poorly that a number of railway enthusiasts turned up to see it and were, not surprisingly, annoyed by being misled.) It must at the same time convey a newly kindled enthusiasm for the work. Too many arts programmes convey the feeling that events are being presented as a kind of public duty ('They liked it in Edinburgh so we may as well try it out here.'), but better written promotions convey the feeling that the administrator's own enthusiasm for the work runs high ('We wanted to have this in our arts centre as soon as possible.'). Promotional material, bearing in mind that the arts administrator should always be open to surprises, must not limit a work's potential audience by implying that it is really only suitable for people who are well bred/highly educated/deeply knowledgeable/only interested in the avant garde/heterosexual, or whatever.

Promotion can of course take many other forms. The venue's other amenities may be promoted as the major attraction, with the art apparently secondary. Thus a campaign for the V & A gallery in London in 1987/8 promoted it as 'an Ace Caff with a Gallery attached'. Or an artist's work may be promoted 'on the back of' promotion for another product, as with Dewars' Scotch 'profiles'. Again, it may be promoted in one medium by means of another, as sales of classic novels such as *Middlemarch* or *Jane Eyre* are boosted by their television or film adaptations.

More subtly, an arts event may sometimes be promoted by 'selling the audience to itself'. Many a mediocre performance has been boosted by announcing that it will take place 'in the presence of' somebody who is assumed to shed such lustre on the event that questions about the quality of the show become irrelevant. And an arts activity or event may also be promoted by additional inducements. For example, the concert seasons at Birmingham's botanical gardens were for many years promoted as musical evenings which centered around a buffet and wine, while all purchasers of subscriptions to Repertory Theatre seasons in the same city found they had entered a grand draw with a 'fabulous holiday' as first prize.

Promotions can be much more straightforward, however. A visiting circus may give each shopkeeper displaying their posters a pile of advertising slips which give 'two seats for the price of one' at early performances. Specific party concessions to targeted groups and societies are a common form of promotion. More generally, interest can be aroused by carefully staged promotional 'stunts'. Houdini for example would plaster the town in which he was to appear with posters offering various 'challenges' to the local townspeople, which, like all good promotional stunts, would attract the interest of local reporters and so multiply the promotion's effectiveness. Remembering that nothing attracts crowds like the whiff of danger, in recent years publicists have sometimes staged 'dangerous accidents' at late rehearsals for a spectacular show. These are then publicized, promoting the show, Houdini-like, by drawing attention to the huge risks the daring performers take.

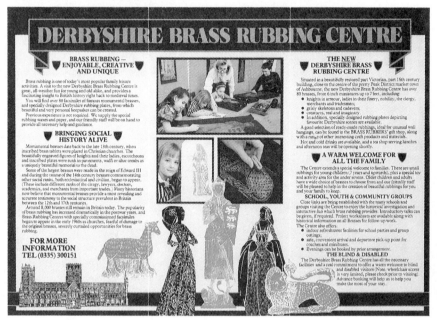

Figure 4 An example of good promotional writing

c) Accessibility

The arts event is not available to all those who are given information about it. Some will not have the means of transporting themselves to the event; others may not have sufficient money to buy a ticket; others may have other engagements. And of those for whom the event is theoretically available, many will conclude that it is nevertheless inaccessible, for despite its availability they cannot see themselves drawing pleasure and benefit from it.

An event may be inaccessible for obvious reasons. It may be that the prospective attender does not even know enough about the art form to render the work meaningful, let alone pleasurable. It may be that the prospect of being amongst the kind of people who seem to enjoy the work is forbidding enough to prevent attendance at the event. It may be (as the authors discovered was the case when researching children's reaction to watching full-scale opera) that the conventions and coded language of booking are sufficiently daunting to prevent some people from attending.

It is an error to imagine, as 'cultural economists' sometimes aver, that people decide whether or not to go to an arts event simply by balancing the pleasure they will get from the event against the price of a ticket. The act of varying ticket prices does not always have an impact, and where there is an identifiable effect it is sometimes quite contrary to expectations. Increasing prices can on occasion increase demand, and lowering prices can sometimes depress it. More often, the price is not the prime determinant of attendance.

A person's decision to attend is of course determined in large part by the art work itself, but is also shaped by:

- perception of the sort of people who will be attending;
- whether they can comfortably go alone, or whether they will be better accompanied by family or friends who enhance the visit;
- the quality of the amenities in and around the event, such as parking, safety in the nearby streets, the restaurant and bars, comfortable areas for meeting friends in, and the absence of social tension. The latter shows up in much research on people's attitudes to public spaces; there are some which by their lighting, furniture and appointments suggest a particular class association, and many do not 'feel easy' in such surroundings.

Of all these points perhaps the most neglected is the question of whether people prefer to go alone or in groups. The work of an occupational pyschologist, Alec Bruce (1982), is important here. In work on audiences for various events at the London Institute of Contemporary Arts, he showed up an interesting variation on how sociable people are when visiting different art forms (Table 7.1).

Table 7.1 Sociability of people using different art forms

	Cinema	Theatre	Exhibitions	Concerts
People solo	370	160	424	294
People in pairs	430	434	452	500
People in threes or more	200	356	132	210
% men	60.0	52.8	53.0	62.0

The desire to be in a group when visiting a theatre or concert hall would seem, on this evidence, to be much stronger than when visiting a gallery or cinema, both of which people seem happier to visit alone. In his work Bruce has gone further and, using techniques known as 'Markov sequences' has created a model for the ways in which people may choose whether they will actually go to an arts event, according to whether (if they are not minded to go alone) they can persuade family or friends to accompany them. It is suggested by these means that one in five people who want to go to an arts event do not do so because they cannot persuade the desired friends or family to accompany them.

This leads to a further point. The accessibility of an arts event is shaped not just by such obvious details as the date, location and price of admission, but also by the general ambience of the venue, and by the efforts made to promote group visits. Extensive work on the composition of West End audiences, for instance, has shown that first-time visitors to the theatre are most likely to come in groups (Gardiner, 1986), and a marketing strategy must therefore include promotion of visits by societies and groups of all kinds. It is equally important that an arts marketer looks hard at the reasons people may have for **not** wishing to come to a venue, alone or with friends. Are the foyers scruffy, with poor cloakroom facilities? Are there places where a single person can stand or sit comfortably, and are there places where groups can comfortably gather? Is there a range of food, drink and other merchandise on sale which does not prejudge the character of the audience? Some people may not want to eat chocolate and popcorn while watching a film, and others may like to drink tea during an evening interval. Is it warm in winter, and air conditioned in summer? Is there an unpleasant cacophony of sound, or unpleasant smells, from the activities of cleaners and bar stockers, or from the kitchens? Above all, do all the staff make all kinds of visitor welcome, whether they are coming to see a show or simply idling?

The most important factor in publicity is always 'word of mouth'. There are two aspects of this: the first is the reputation of the artist and the art work. The second is the reputation of the venue in which it is performed or exhibited. Some may think that advertising a gallery by means of its 'ace caff' is faintly demeaning to art, but the truth is that a gallery which looks with suspicion on shabbily dressed single visitors, or a theatre with poor bar and catering services is itself demeaning to art, by rendering it less accessible.

7.2 RESOURCES FOR MARKETING

Marketing an arts programme is expensive. A medium-scale arts centre, concert hall or theatre will probably advertise on radio, occasionally on television, regularly in ten or fifteen newspapers, in twenty or thirty magazines and brochures, and in addition will generate fifty or more printed layouts each year in the form of posters, fliers, hanging cards, car stickers, mail shots and brochures. Few such centres will have a marketing budget of less than £100 000 a year, and many will spend much more.

An overall marketing strategy, however, depends on much more than spending money on printed material, and assembling resources involves much more than arguing for an increased advertising budget. Two of the most important resources are a) detailed knowledge of your potential audience, and b) constant assessment of the marketing programme.

Knowledge as resource

Anyone marketing an arts programme in Britain will need to know in detail the composition and nature of the population living within thirty to thirty-five miles of the venue. In larger countries with different transport infrastructures that notional 'market radius' may be very different. Additionally, they will need to be familiar with the patterns of local tourism (when the locals go on holiday as well as when visitors may arrive), local transport timetables, the marketing of all other local attractions which may suggest 'packages' (p.101 below) and a good deal of local history. The reason for the last suggestion may not be obvious. The fact is that arts administrators frequently work in relatively unfamiliar places and may for example not recognize that an intended joke is giving offence for hidden local reasons, or that there is a local reason for an otherwise inexplicable falling-away of support. (Some years ago in a small East Midlands town, a repertory company was horrified to see attendances drop away dramatically in September, after the management thought they had won substantial local support. Nobody had told them how important it was to get the harvest in while there was still some evening light.)

The marketer needs a constantly updated list of media contacts (everywhere from television newsrooms to parish newsletters) who can 'spread the word' at the appropriate time for each work. Most important perhaps is that the arts marketer should also have a coded list of key people (society secretaries, community group leaders, social club organizers, school music and drama teachers) who can be readily contacted at appropriate times and bring in group bookings. But such people must not be used indiscriminately. The arts marketer should have sufficient local knowledge to realize which of the group 'organizers' are likely to be interested in which work, and should only contact them on that basis. It is fatal to distribute promotional material too generally, particularly if the work is being offered so cheaply that it is obvious you are 'papering the house', as this will destroy the element of trust. Equally disastrous is the implied moral imperative, that right-thinking people 'ought' to support a local venue, however uninteresting its offerings, simply because it is there. Instead the band of 'organizers' should be encouraged to feel they are being offered something excellent to which they will want to come out of desire rather than duty. Ideally, even if the arts marketer's list has several hundred names on it, each group organizer should feel that he or she has a special relationship with the venue.

Assessment

A great deal of money is wasted on marketing because of the ignorance of arts managements. For example, they may spend heavily on printing hundreds of posters for each event without ever discovering whether posters play a significant part in attracting an audience. Or they may regularly mail out brochures to a poorly-constructed, out-of-date list of addresses. Or they may live in ignorance of what deters people from attending their shows because they have never surveyed their potential market. Almost as damaging, they may remain ignorant of how much more time and money attenders are willing to spend in the venue, because they have never asked, for example, whether people would like to book ticket, car-parking space, programme and refreshments in one transaction.

A part of the marketing budget must always be set aside for surveying and assessment. For marketing surveys, the arts marketer may use an expert consultancy, such as the ETB PIN Marketing Service, to map out the potential audience, and this must be supplemented from time to time by attitude surveys amongst those who do *not* visit the venue. If carefully planned, some assessment can be carried out in-house. A systematic sample of attenders (created, for example, by asking every fifth person to come through the doors on certain selected days to respond to a questionnaire) can be asked a number of key questions: why they have come to this show, how much they have spent on the trip, what transport they used, what size of group they have come with, what attracts them in the forthcoming programme, what sort of thing they would like to see included, and what criticisms and suggestions they may have.

However, careful planning of such assessments is essential. Expert advice needs to be sought on the layout of any questionnaire, as well as on the interpretation of the results. Too many surveys ask banal questions which imply the answer ('Would you like to see more musical comedies, more classic dramas or more documentaries?') and too many ask questions which can be answered by other means. For example, it is pointless asking people how much they spent on drinks in the venue's bars when all that is needed is an aggregate sum, which is instantly available from the bar takings. Equally, there is little point in asking people their mode of transport if the great majority of visitors' cars are left in one paying car park by the venue, figures for which are readily available. People cannot be asked to respond to questionnaires too often, so it is important, when one is undertaken, to get it right.

Much information can of course be gathered by the staff, without setting up a questionnaire survey. Discreet observation undertaken by unpaid helpers can give important information about times of audience arrival and departure, about the adequacy of cloakroom facilities, or how many people gave up trying to buy interval refreshments in overcrowded foyers. Advance booking forms attached to mail shots can be colour-coded so that the box office will know which areas support which kinds of show – without the embarrassment of having to ask people for their address or postal code. The reception counter or ticket office can make rapid notes on categories of customer, which are sometimes useful. As we have already noted, it is helpful to know the average number of tickets bought at any one purchase. *Cats*, for instance, is a regular sell-out, not least because people come in large groups to see it – the average number of tickets sold in each purchase is usually around seven. It is also helpful to know whether the majority of customers are men or women, old or young, white or black, and how it varies from show to show. The times of all telephone bookings can be logged so that more staff are engaged at the peak times. Changes in attendance during school holidays, spells of good weather, during periods of recession or when there is a national celebration (a Royal Wedding for example) should also be carefully noted, all as a part of the ongoing assessment of the market.

7.3 PACKAGING AND PRESENTATION

In an increasingly bureaucratic milieu the arts administrator is tempted to spend more time in presenting an organization's work in a form acceptable to the funders than in presenting it positively to the general public. As a result, the public image of subsidized arts organizations is often that of poverty-stricken, unworldly gatherings of well-meaning people obsessed with political correctness rather than with excitement and pleasure. The programmes and the façades of arts venues are sometimes embellished with appeals for funds rather than with advertisements for art. Newspaper reports relegate reviews of the arts programme to the back pages but lead with the seemingly endless political turmoil over funds. The excitement conveyed is thus not in the artistic programme but in the political and economic turmoil of survival. In this, as in so many respects, arts administration is holistic in nature. If the image conveyed on a newspaper's leading pages is of a municipal facility embroiled in local politics then no amount of slick 'marketing' will dislodge that unfortunate impression.

Indeed the difference between the dour image of some state-subsidized venues and the kind of glitzy presentation still favoured by circus showmen is illuminating. The façades of some subsidized arts venues convey a notion of service, worthy improvement and political correctness. By contrast the painted circus 'front' of Chipperfields or Cottle's suggests colour, danger, beauty and excitement. There is about the state-aided venue generally an air of deserving charity, set amidst bureaucratic gentility. Everything carries the logos of the grant-aiding bodies, and inscribed panels thank corporations for their financial support. Consequently the funders seem sometimes to matter more than the paying public. By contrast the circus simply boasts about how many paying customers flock in to it. Even if the proprietor is having a rough time, he or she is always seen wearing 'the flash', at the wheel of an expensive car, and with a glamorous wagon in the background – the very opposite of the 'begging bowl posture' which state-funded organizations sometimes adopt (Pick, Ajala and Anderton, 1988).

The image the public forms of any arts programme is compounded of many things: the reputation of the artists, the critical reception afforded to the work, the venue and its amenities, the price of admission – some are obvious enough. But that image is also formed by a whole series of other impressions – the kind of people seen going in and out of the venue, the photographs of dignitaries which appear in the newspapers, and the kinds of event which are not presented there. As we emphasize in our discussion of holistic management (Chapter 9 below), the arts administrator needs to be alive to the total effect of all the ways in which the organization presents itself to the public. If people seem to dress up to make an advance booking, if the press photographs are always of local toffs opening exhibitions and making speeches and if the programme contains no popular entertainer or nothing of interest to local cooks, dressmakers, DIY fanatics or gardeners, then it is of little use wasting time on making fine populist statements in the brochures. The public at large will see clearly enough that the programme is elitist in tone and of marginal interest, and that the advertising ('This is YOUR arts centre') is merely designed to impress the funding bodies.

One way of countering a false impression of elitism is by astute 'packaging' – that is, by selling a 'package' which does not isolate and erect barriers around an arts activity, but links it with various other leisure activities. An arts venue will seem much less forbidding if it is one of fifteen places which people can visit when they have bought a 'visitor's card' for the area, or if owning a ticket for a performance in it means you can travel free to and from the venue on public transport. The members of the family who waver over a theatre visit will be convinced if a family 'party ticket' includes a good meal, drink and theatre seats. Young couples will be much likelier to attend if the concert package includes a baby-sitting service. Older people will be much more probable attenders if there is cheap transport and safe escort home. Visitors to the area will be pleased if there is a mid-week package which offers half-price seats together with their hotel booking. The arts marketer needs to keep a constant stream of packaged offers available – remembering that they not only swell the attendance figures but, equally importantly, soften any impression that the arts venue 'belongs' to a privileged clique.

7.4 REACHING AUDIENCES

We need to reach our prospective audience in three ways: with information about the programme, by promotion of events and activities which will interest particular segments of it, and by making it easy to book tickets. Until quite recently the three things could not be done together. Arts administrators had to hope that the public's desire to come to the show, roused by various promotional stunts, would be sustained until they had the opportunity to visit the box office.

Now it is technically possible to mail prospective attenders directly with promotional material which invites them to pick up a phone and simply make their booking, by credit card, on a 24-hour reservation line. If the marketer has well-researched information, a prospective audience thought likely to enjoy a particular work can be 'targeted'.

In Britain such targeting is sometimes achieved by using a system known as ACORN (A Classification of Residential Neighbourhoods). This system was created in the early 1980s, when data from the 1981 census was loaded on to giant computers, and from it 38 different 'types' were created (based on size of the family, type of housing, number of cars owned, and so on). As census data are gathered from enumeration zones of around 150 households, and because those zones tend to represent a particular postcode, it is usually possible to tell anyone's ACORN type from their postcode, or to tell what proportion of types live within one postcoded area.

Research in the mid-eighties further showed that arts attenders usually come from ACORN types I, J and K – single professional people, affluent families and better-off retired families. Other systems, such as VALS (Values and Lifestyle Segmentation), also point to the fact that well-off, well-educated and socially-aware people are more immediately likely to be arts attenders than are other, less advantaged, groups.

So it could be said that such tools told arts marketers nothing they did not already know – except perhaps where their 'targets' could most readily be found, and in broad terms what kinds of overall response could be predicted for a particular presentation. Yet ACORN has proved useful in allowing marketers effectively to target groups that are not already dedicated arts attenders; there have for example been several examples of organizations which have used ACORN to target low income or single parent families (not normally arts attenders) and, by the provision of crèche or baby-sitting facilities, greatly increase their attendance.

Yet the fact remains that, unless a target has been identified, it is an expensive and chancey matter to reach an audience effectively. In Britain it costs about 33p a household to mail a coloured promotional brochure to it, 40p if the total cost of maintaining the necessary 24-hour reservation lines is added in. As experience shows that there is only one success in 400 from 'cold' selling by mail, then the grim conclusion is that each ticket sold would probably be costing around £160 in marketing costs!

7.5 SELLING

It is a great attraction to the marketer to sell a series of tickets to each purchaser, so that the costs of each ticket sale are far less. One way of doing this is through the old eighteenth century method of selling subscriptions to a 'season' of concerts, operas or plays. The advantages of subscription selling include much lower costs relative to each ticket sale, and giving the presenter box office money 'up front' at the start of the season. The disadvantages include the necessity to present a full 'package' for a season well in advance, which involves the risk that the season will be arranged predominantly to suit a particular clientele, and that new, challenging work may be jettisoned in the interests of the 'package'. It also means that the administration runs the risk of a catastrophic fall in sales when some important artiste – for example a popular conductor – withdraws. Perhaps the commonest objection is that subscription selling can be too successful, giving the impression of a 'closed shop'. For arts marketers need to sell both to the known arts attenders (the 'insiders'), and additionally to those people in other categories who might draw pleasure and benefit from a work. This means that our promotional material and our 'packages' must be constantly directed to a succession of 'outside' groups. It means that pricing must be in constant flux, with concessions and special rates ensuring that price is not automatically a bar to any such 'outsiders'. It means also that our selling must be through systems which the prospective audience member is familiar with, and in a place and form which is readily and continuously accessible.

There should be as many points of sale as possible, and selling should be via the largest possible number of means. In addition to ticket sales through the venue's own desks, prospective customers should be able to reserve tickets in shops and stores in surrounding towns and villages, make postal bookings (on order forms mailed to them, or printed in local newspapers), and make telephone bookings on 24-hour lines. An enterprising arts marketer will soon recognize further opportunities. There can be mobile ticket booths in local caravan parks, visiting local markets and fairs, tokens delivered with the milk which can be exchanged for half-price tickets, tickets sold in pubs and clubs, exchangeable vouchers in wage packets, tickets on sale in garages and bought as you pay for the petrol, coupons in holiday brochures, or 'family price' vouchers given to each person buying a season ticket for the winter's football or ice hockey. Once it is accepted that more points of sale mean proportionately larger audiences and probably much livelier audiences too, then many new possibilities open up.

Such a flexible range of selling points, and such fluidity over pricing is only possible when the venue's ticket sales are fully computerized. A good computerized ticketing system comprises:

- A microprocessor memory file which stores full details of venue seating, and instantly updates information on seats sold, discounted etc. for each performance, as soon as a sale is made.
- Video terminals which instantly display the seating plan for any performance updated to the point of the last sale, and which interrogate the memory file to select seats.
- A ticket printer, or printers, which produce the ticket as soon as the transaction is recorded.
- A printer which produces returns, accounting and statistical data on sales as required.

Systems can be purely in-house, or linked together in groups to sell tickets for several venues. Or an agency system may be preferred (Reid, 1983):

With an 'agency' system, an independent company with a central computer sets up a network of terminals selling tickets for many different ... forms of entertainment. The ticket selling points can be located in shops, travel agencies, theatre box offices etc. Such a system is financed by a commission fee on every ticket sold.

It is doubtful whether any arts venue could now long survive in Britain if it did not match its leisure industry rivals' range of selling points, so the uncomputerized box office is becoming very rare.

Two of the initial anxieties about computerization have been overcome. The information stored in the memory file has been shown to be safe. It cannot be accidentally 'lost', and only those with the access codes can extract any part of it. Moreover, computers do not dehumanize the box office. Indeed, as they leave the ticket sales staff free to serve the customer more quickly, with less tiresome paperwork and with less possibility of error, they should make polite and friendly service easier to achieve.

By tradition, booking in theatres and concert halls is logged either as 'advance' (usually comprising tickets sold up to about 24 hours before the performance) or 'doors' (tickets sold in the hours leading up to the performance). Many commercial venues book all seats up to a year ahead, so their returns consist entirely of the 'advance', but in some state-aided venues a few seats in the 'advance' for each performance are deliberately left unbooked so that there are some left for sale on the 'doors'. By these means the general public does not feel totally excluded. Students, tourists and chance visitors can thus come along on the day and have some chance of a seat.

The administrator has to advertise seat prices before the box office opens, and cannot readily change them if he or she discovers that there is a much greater demand for the seats at £20 than he or she suspected, a much lower demand for the £30 seats, and no demand at all for the £10 ones. The administrator has then only two devices, the first being to fall back on what old fairground showmen used to call 'moving the rope'. The phrase comes from the time when showmen such as Richardson and Wombwell presented shows in large tented booths. Admission to the rear of the tent's auditorium was through one entrance and cost a penny. Admission to the front portion was through another entrance and cost twopence. The two parts of the audience were separated by a rope. If the queue on the twopenny side were larger, they would quickly 'move the rope' inside the tent to make a larger arena at the front – although some of the twopenny audience would then be standing on ground they could have occupied for a penny, if that queue had been the larger. In the same way, seeing that there is high demand for one price band, the arts administrator can reprogramme the box office computer so that some of the seats formerly priced at an unrealizable £30 are now sold at £20, at which price there is substantial demand.

The second device, used in London and New York, is to sell off remaining seats at half price in ticket booths located in the heart of the tourist area. Some managements will not join in the scheme, and participating managements which have seats to sell insist that their availability is not made too public. So people queuing tend to learn quite late, from a small notice, which shows are selling cheap seats that day, and there is no indication what may be on sale on subsequent days. It does, however, fill theatres for shows that may be going through a difficult time temporarily. And for most managements selling 'half-price' is worthwhile, even though it cuts something from the receipts. By contrast an unsold seat is an irretrievable loss.

REFERENCES

Bruce, A. (1983) 'A model of audience formation', in *Economic Research in the Performing Arts* (1983).

Coward, N. (1982) *Diaries*.

Diggle, K. (1994) 'Back to first principles', in *Arts Management Weekly* (March 1994).

Gardiner, C. (1986) *The West End Theatre Audience 1985/6*.

Pick, J. with Ajala, R. and Anderton, M. (1988) *The Arts in a State*.

Reid, F. (1983) *Theatre Administration*.

Development of arts audiences

8.1 ARTS AUDIENCES

Inevitably, we have concentrated in recent chapters upon the arts audience that is most visible, the audience that gathers in a public venue. Yet, elsewhere, there is a larger arts audience, beyond the immediate control of the arts administrator. That is the audience which listens to music on radio, tapes and compact disc, which enjoys drama at home in the form of the classic TV serial or the rented video, and which looks at prints and photographs, not in a gallery, but on the walls of the living room. For the same reason, readers of the 60 000 and more new books that are published in Britain each year also tend to be ignored when 'arts audiences' are counted, because people generally read books at home, and not in a public place where they can form part of an economic statistic. Yet, however difficult it may be accurately to quantify domestic arts activity, it is certainly the case in Britain that many more people enjoy the arts in their own homes than in public venues, and that this is at least as important a part of 'the arts' as the public activities regularly tabulated in official statistics.

Although the arts administrator may control events far less completely, it is still a duty, insofar as is possible, to create conditions for an aesthetic contract, bringing the art into contact, domestically and privately, with a 'proper' audience. The good arts administrator will not, for instance, use a falsely alluring book-jacket. (The authors recall seeing a youth excitedly opening a paperback book on a train. It featured on the cover a waif gazing besottedly into the cleavage of a tightly corseted woman above the phrase 'The boy who wanted more ...'. After a couple of pages the puzzled youth put down the book. It was *Oliver Twist*.) Nor will the good arts administrator promote compact discs, tapes or videos which have deliberately misleading covers or falsely titillating promotional material, because the artists are ill-served by such devices and the work will remain unheard or, in the case of *Oliver Twist* described above, unread. It is also bad business. For instance, there is considerable evidence to show that if, in 'book clubs', the customer has been falsely lured into thinking that a particular kind of literature will give 'hours of pleasure', the take-up rate of people extending their membership into a second year is less than 4%.

There are some areas, of course, in which artists reach vast publics without direct involvement by any arts administrator. Of these the most overwhelmingly important is advertising. 'The magic system' in all its forms uses artists as creators and performers. For many artists it is a prime source of revenue (Pick and Anderton, 1992). For some modern critics commercials and short TV 'stings' are art. Certainly, as Judith Williamson (1986) shows, the relationship between advertising and known art is complicated:

> Unlike advertising, Art has a reputation for being above things vulgar and mercenary, a form eternal rather than social, whose appreciation springs from the discerning heart, not the cultural background. This ethereal notion can be brought down with a bump by the merest glimpse, on the one hand at the Art market, distinguished from other fields of commercial gain only by the intriguing fact that it successfully deals in the 'priceless', and on the other hand, at that equally effective cultural economy whereby anything that too many people like is rapidly devalued as 'art'. Classical music which makes it onto '100 Favourites' LPs becomes scorned by 'serious' music lovers; reproductions even of valued paintings, like Van Gogh's 'Sunflowers', disappear from the walls of the cognoscenti when they become widely enough loved to be sold at Woolworth's.

> It is on this 'cultural economy' that advertising feeds its endless appetite for social values. Ads are in the business not of creating, but of recycling social categories, relying on systems of value already in existence as sources for the 'auras', at once tangible and precise, which must be associated with the goods for sale. Any system which is already structured in terms of up-market and down-market is especially useful, the more so if it has a high investment in denying its own workings. Advertising pitches its products at specific social classes (carefully graded from A to E) yet, as with Art, choice and taste must appear as personal attributes for the individual. So 'Art' is a particularly appropriate system for ads: while appearing to be 'above' social distinctions, it provides a distinct set of social codes we all understand.

> For what is interesting is the degree of agreement at both ends of the social scale as to what 'Art' is. Art is felt to be 'difficult', its meaning not accessible to everyday use of the perceptive faculties. It is something which the great majority of people feel is somehow above them, out of reach and beyond their grasp. This perfectly mirrors the opinion of those select few who can be assured of their good taste simply by its exclusiveness.

This offers the interesting view that advertising does not so much subvert the arts with its commercialism as reinforce stereotypes of art, art genres and arts lovers. The arts administrator's marketing, which is often attempting to break down such stereotyped images, must then sometimes work against advertising in general.

Williamson's analysis is also useful in another sense. It helps to remind us that some of the people who watch advertisements, who follow *Eastenders*, gamble, go to the supermarket, or watch football, will also enjoy serious drama, the opera or modern art. One of the marketing discoveries of the 1980s was that although in a majority of cases the other leisure activities of arts audiences are predictable, a satisfactorily large minority of them do not conform to type. Some readers of *The Sun* do enjoy Mozart. Some readers of *The Times* enjoy Led Zeppelin. Users of Persil enjoy Jim Davidson and Nola Rae. From a representative quota sample of 1230 people interviewed throughout Britain, Jacobs and Worcester (1991) came to these conclusions about arts audiences:

- **Opera** Among opera-goers, seven in ten had also been to a theatre (74%) and a museum (73%). Six in ten had been to a cinema or art exhibition (61%); one in four to a pop concert (27%) and one in five to a football match (20%) or a classical ballet (21%).
- **Pop concerts** Nearly eight in ten of those who went to a pop concert also went to the cinema (77%) and more than six in ten (64%) to a library. One in three went to a football match and about the same number to an art exhibition.
- **Library** Library users take part in other activities more than the average: 38% of the population went to museums but 52% of library-users did so; 23% of the population went to art galleries but 33% of library users did.

The participants were asked to look at a list of arts activities and to say which they had been to in the previous 12 months. The complete list shows the percentage of visitors to each:

Library	53%
Cinema	44%
National Trust house/garden	39%
Museum	38%
Theatre	36%
Art exhibition	23%
Football match	19%
Pop concert	17%
Pantomime	15%
Orchestral concert	14%
Modern dance	13%
Opera	6%
Classical ballet	3%

The work showed that what some had regarded as up-market pursuits – visiting National Trust properties, museums, theatres and art exhibitions – greatly exceeded football and pop (widely regarded as the mass public entertainments of the day) in the breadth of their appeal.

Of more value to arts administrators was the fact that the supposed 'cultural snobbery' of high art lovers was revealed as a myth. Opera and ballet buffs showed the greatest breadth of cultural interests. They, the supposed 'snobs', were far more likely to be seen at a football match than a football fan was likely to be seen at the opera.

There is then no such thing as a discrete 'arts audience' which reserves leisure time exclusively for enjoying the arts in public venues. As we have stressed throughout the book, there are only a series of interlinked audiences, some public, many domestic, which are interlinked with each other and with participants in, and audiences for, all other kinds of leisure activity. So, as the administrator nurtures and develops audiences he or she must be careful not to fall into the stereotypes conveyed by advertising. The image conveyed of the arts activity – the associations, images and language by which the arts are 'placed' – must be rigorously and regularly reassessed. And, as every management student knows, the internal language of the organization should be scrutinized as carefully as the external language of advertising. (The authors remember with pleasure a researcher who suggested that the audience for a large national arts institution in Britain could as effectively be analysed by psychoanalysing the management as by surveying the paying customers.) In developing arts audiences the good arts administrator will frequently be undermining the insistent stereotypes of the wider advertising industry, remembering that the next generation of theatre lovers is as likely to come from the ranks of rugby players as from fine art connoisseurs. It is sad that when some administrators survey the kind of audience that Hull Truck's touring version of John Godber's *Bouncers* attracts – young people from the C1 and C2 groups who drink lager instead of gin and tonic – they say 'I don't know where this audience has come from' (Murdin, 1994).

8.2 TOURISM

Fifteen years ago it was possible to convey an optimistic picture of tourism and the benefits it brought to the arts. The conventional view was that arts attractions brought high-spending tourists into locations which benefited economically from their spending. There were some anxieties about the overcrowding and pollution tourism seemed to bring, but they were usually brushed aside by organizations such as the British Tourist Authority (1979):

> Every industry operates at some cost to the environment. The congestion, visual intrusion and noise which tourists may cause can be and are

minimised by crowd and traffic control, by selective promotion, by differential pricing and by good physical planning, such as the creation of pedestrian precincts. Tourist interests support such measures in the best interests of tourism.

While the argument of congestion gains a hearing there is little appreciation of the benefits of tourism in combating loneliness in remote areas.

Little has been heard since then of the companionship tourism brings to lonely sherpas and sheep farmers, but much has been heard of the earlier argument. Complaints about the congestion, visual intrusion and noise tourism brings have themselves been getting louder. There has been a loss of faith that selective promotion, differential pricing or good physical planning can do much to rescue such centres as Venice, Stratford-upon-Avon or Bruges from the depredations of their visitors. Planner's schizophrenia, which means that as you approach almost any European town or city you are simultaneously assaulted by signs urging you to take the by-pass round it, and to drive into the centre and spend heavily in the tourist attractions, has become more marked.

Some known tourist venues have taken drastic action. In Athens tourists are no longer allowed to walk around the Parthenon; in Britain tourists are no longer allowed to wander round Stonehenge. The village of Downham, fed up with tourists, urged the authorities to remove it altogether from their publications. There were protests by some neighbourhoods at being linked with artists whom the tourist authorities thought were selling points. Some of the citizens of Eastwood, for example, held public protests at the opening of the D.H. Lawrence Birthplace Museum. There was indignation at some of the ways 'the arts' prostituted themselves before tourists: stories of 'traditional' aboriginal boomerangs being shortened so they could be fitted into jiffy bags for tourists to post home, 'traditional dances' being created by tourism promoters for display in international festivals, bogus 'living museums' which peddled picture postcard notions of a country's history to amuse the visitors.

Media mythologies became disturbingly intertwined with living cultures. Jersey Tourism lost no opportunity to exploit the fact that the TV series *Bergerac* was set on their island. Thousands of tourists visited a pleasant but unremarkable Yorkshire mill town because it was *Last of the Summer Wine* country, and the locals obligingly renamed some of their local cafes and traditional produce after details invented for the TV sitcom. Farmers' leaders made appearances in the BBC radio's fictitious farming series *The Archers*, and the actors made 'real-life' appearances giving advice, amongst other things, on country traditions and farmhouse cooking. Some people said that as the real and media cultures increasingly interwove, and the various Disneylands came to resemble small countries, Britain should give itself over completely to tourism and become one vast theme park.

The argument for 'developing' precincts, inner cities and vast tracts of countryside, simply for the purposes of attracting profitable tourists, has been widely heard in recent years. Usually it is presented as if a government's sole interest in promoting the arts must be commercial. It is not infrequently supported by 'impact studies' which purport to show that the overall spending generated by, for example, attracting tourists to a new arts festival – that is, spending in local hotels, bars, restaurants, transport services, etc. – means that overall, investment in arts facilities which attract tourists yields handsome profits.

However, such impact studies have their weaknesses. When calculating the 'profits' by these means the considerable costs of building new roads, parks, hotels and arenas are sometimes falsely amortized across several years of public expenditure, and no calculation is made of the 'displacement factor' whereby local transport is disrupted, local retailers are sidelined and many locals leave the area to spend their money somewhere else because of the noise and crowds the new festival attracts. There is also a considerable 'knock on' effect on local cultural activities which are not part of the mainstream festival. For example, local arts administrators in Vancouver calculated it was at least three years before they regained their local patronage after the disruptive effects of *Expo 86*.

It is wise to look at the commercial value of tourism by different means. Another kind of analysis is known as a 'base line' impact study. This does not look simply at the spending generated by a new cultural attraction, but looks rather more at where the money ends up – that is, who actually gets the profits. By this second, more sophisticated, analysis one cannot claim that the spending of tourists at a new arts festival is generating profits for the locality, if the money spent is actually enriching far distant corporations who own the local hotels, restaurants, transport services, etc.

The truth is that encouraging tourism sometimes brings disadvantages, and that some of these disadvantages are economic. Britain's own experience gives us useful evidence of this. In 1979 Britain's 'tourist account' (the balance between what incoming tourists spend in Britain and the British spend abroad) showed a slight profit. In 1980 it began to go into the red. By 1982 11 600 000 visitors to Britain spent £3 184 000 000 while Britons made 20 600 000 trips overseas and spent £3 650 000 000 – an overall loss of £466 000 000. Making the usual assumption that cultural spending is about 4% of total tourist spending, the net loss to the arts on that year was some £20 million. In each succeeding year the loss on the 'tourist account' has inexorably risen, and now stands at more than £3.6 billion a year, representing an annual net cultural loss to Britain of some £150 000 000.

Intermingled with these rather gloomy figures are the loss-making effects of 'benefit tourism'. This term, first coined in the seventies, alludes to those persons who enter a country with a highly developed welfare state ostensibly as tourists, but who claim welfare benefits during their stay, and who pay no tax. In Britain it is reckoned that such benefit tourists, who sometimes claim social security and health benefits during extended stays, cost the country £30 million in 1994/5.

For many arts administrators however the real argument about tourism lies more in cost benefit analysis, which looks at the cultural harm tourists may do. They will look at the cultural phenomenon known as 'falsification by tourism', which occurs when theatres simplify their dramatic, dance and musical offerings simply to please tourists; when galleries show art works more to do with cultural PR than with the statements real artists are making; when museums selectively show artefacts that harmonize with the picture the tourist authorities want to give rather than with the truth. It can then be said that even if the country's tourism account shows a net profit, something else, at least as valuable as the balance of payments, is still being destroyed.

Of course it would be foolish to say that an arts administrator should not try to attract visitors from as wide an international catchment as is possible. Those efforts must be made. The arts must not, however, be restyled simply as items of cultural diplomacy, or as baubles to boost the trading account. The point at which such damage is caused is when visitors begin to be treated quite differently because they are 'tourists'. If the programme is changed, cut or simplified for them, if works are detached from their cultural context to be sold to them, or they are received with condescension, as potential buyers rather than as people presenting the administrator with a new challenge to form a good aesthetic contract, then the arts administrator is failing and has, in a useful American phrase, 'sold out'.

In fact the distant visitor often provides real opportunities for enlarging audiences, without any need of falsifying the nature of the arts. Although we look carefully at the habits of visitors to our own countries, we perhaps pay too little attention to what our compatriots enjoy while abroad, and do not 'match up' cultural spending at home with that abroad. For we have different cultural and spending patterns when on holiday. US visitors to Britain, for example, go far more often to the theatre when on vacation than they do at home. A much higher proportion of British visitors to Moscow go to the ballet than do at home. Over a half of all adult museum visits are made when on holiday. There is no indication that most people away from home expect to be short-changed, and they will rightly be annoyed if they are. The arts administrator must take full advantage of efforts to promote tourism, but must avoid pandering to the stereotyped notion of the unreceptive, uncomprehending tourist.

8.3 PRICING AND SPENDING

We have also suggested that in some areas of the arts the traditional supply and demand curves which supposedly govern prices in the open market actually work in reverse. Because the appeal of some arts events, or of owning some art works, lies in their exclusivity to the purchaser, raising prices sometimes increases demand. Conversely, reducing prices may decrease demand, because it is thereby felt to be less valuable artistically as well as economically. And, as we have already said, pricing is in any case rarely the sole determinant of whether someone chooses to visit an arts event or not, so either raising or lowering prices may, according to the other determinants, sometimes have contrary effects or none at all.

Important reinforcement of the view that prices were not the major factor in determining demand for performing arts events came with the Millward Brown International Report (1990) on decision-making factors in prospective arts audiences in Britain. Twenty decision-making factors were ranked in importance. As will be seen from the top ten, overall price was considered less important than seven other factors:

Very Important/Important

1.	Quality of performance	95%
2.	That it's entertaining	93%
3.	Subject matter	90%
4.	Ease of booking	82%
5.	Comfort of seats	80%
6.	Actors/singers/musicians/dancers	78%
7.	Choice of different ticket prices	77%
8.	Ticket price	76%
9.	Company/orchestra	74%
10.	Good parking nearby	74%

Two aspects of this report are of particular interest at this point. The first is that 'choice of different ticket prices', i.e. a range of available prices, was considered more important than the ticket prices themselves. The second is that, according to the art form, between 65% and 87% of attenders said they would be willing to pay more for their tickets.

We have thus a further possible objection to blanket state subsidies. If they are applied indiscriminately to all customers we not only have a very large number of people paying less than they are prepared to, but a proportion feeling that the product is being devalued by its low pricing. Countering this, without using some draconian system of cultural needs testing, seems hard.

Yet there is an answer. For other reasons we have several times urged in this book that arts events should always offer a range of admission prices, that there should be a constant flow of special offers designed to attract groups, and a variety of packages, with differential pricing, designed both to attract people at present under-represented in the audience mix, and to induce regular attenders of one kind of event to try another. We have also stressed that separate events should not be priced solely on their costs, but that more cheaply-staged events should 'subsidize' more expensive ones. The prospective customer should therefore be faced with a great variety of packages and prices for each season. The evidence is that this variety, enabling customers to pick a range of events at prices they consider appropriate for them, is now highly rated as a decision-making factor.

The two disastrous ways of pricing are first, simply to calculate pricing for each event by dividing known costs by the number of seats expected to be sold, and second, to charge the 'going rate' for an artist or company. We are suggesting instead that:

- prices are calculated over a period of weeks, or a complete season;
- the range of prices (together with discounts, packages and special offers) for each show is calculated around a median price, yielding a prospective gross income, which does not necessarily relate directly to that show's costs; but that
- the total of prospective gross incomes for the season is so ordered that it yields the required total box office income for the season.

When surveying the prospective price structure and the advertising material for a coming season, the arts administrator will find it useful to imagine, in turn, a range of people looking at it: students, labourers, sportsmen, churchgoers, some rich, some young, some poor, some old, some handicapped, some with large families, some without friends, some busy at work, others unemployed. He, or she, has to imagine each group asking itself two important questions: 'Do I want to come to this?' and 'Have I the means to come?' It is the administrator's job to ensure that as many people as possible say 'yes' to both questions.

REFERENCES

British Tourist Authority (1979) *Tourism in Britain: the Broad Perspective.*
Jacobs, E. and Worcester, R. (1991) *Typically British?.*
Millward Brown International (1990) *Pricing in the Arts.*
Murdin, L. (1994) 'I can't think of a more exciting job', in *Arts Management Weekly* (April 1994).
Pick, J. and Anderton, M. (1992) *Artists and the Arts Industry.*
Williamson, J. (1986) *Consuming Passions: the Dynamics of Popular Culture.*

<table>
<tr><td>**9**</td><td># Arts administration: conclusions</td></tr>
</table>

Until the 1960s it was still not unusual to find arts enterprises which were administrated, yet had no designated administrator. Many weekly reps would keep their financial records 'in a biscuit tin', and, at best, the administration would be done by an assistant stage manager, or a bit-part actor for one day a week. In numerous 'collectives' all administrative decisions were taken by general vote. Pop groups, companies with touring shows, and radical arts groups formed and re-formed casually, often without any clear business agreement; their names, 'The Wildcats', 'John Bull Puncture Repair Kit', 'RAT theatre', 'Foot's Barn', providing a litany to a vanished age.

Increased complexity of licensing, taxation and company law, combined with a less casual and more bureaucratic funding system, led to each state-supported arts organization having to appoint, in the seventies, a named administrator, who carried responsibility for the handling of government funds. The Arts Council, through its long-serving finance director, Anthony Field, took a leading part in the training of such administrators. At the same time, local government developed its own separate but equally rigorous training schemes through the NALGO Correspondence Institute, with examinations for arts and leisure officers administered by the then Institute of Municipal Entertainment. Commercial enterprises, then, as now, the largest sector of 'the arts industry' generally trained their managers 'in-house'.

Thus there was from the start difficulty with the term 'arts administrator'. Though it was used (alongside 'producer', 'manager', 'leader', 'warden', 'promoter' and 'director') within the state-supported arts sector, it was hardly ever used in local government (where it meant a particular kind of secretary) or in the commercial sector. Some people nevertheless were to use the term as generally as we have used it throughout this book (referring to the officer, manager, leader or organizer of any kind of arts project) but others found the term 'arts administrator' a nuisance. They saw administration as a more limited activity than managing. The arts administrator was in their eyes a facilitator and enabler only, while the real power and the right to take decisive entrepreneurial action more properly belonged to a 'director' or 'manager'. Still others, less concerned with confused semantics than with the practicalities of the situation, pointed out that in practice good administrators and creative directors and producers frequently went hand in hand (like Stevens and Neville at the Nottingham Playhouse, or Aukin and Mackintosh at the Leicester Haymarket) and that the arts administrator was in any case usually part of a management team.

In local government the notion that the arts 'administrator' (usually termed an arts or leisure 'officer') was part of a team, in a structure with both vertical and horizontal line management, was generally accepted. Increasingly it became accepted in larger commercial organizations, although some entrepreneurial administrators (such as Mary Chipperfield, John Bloom, Robert Stigwood and Andrew Meadmore) successfully negotiated the seventies and eighties. The day of the 'heroic' administrator was generally thought to have passed, and experts on team management techniques pointed out that many of the best-known entrepreneurs of the past were in fact the public face of what was privately a management team. Walt Disney, for example, took no decisions alone, but relied upon a close management team, in particular his brother Roy (Margerison and McCann, 1991).

So, we have used the term 'arts administrator' throughout to mean a person who, by whatever title, shapes, plans, budgets for, controls and operates any kind of arts venture. We have usually referred, in the singular, to 'him or her' because it was easier to discuss the practices of arts administration in such focused terms. But we must now reiterate what we said at the beginning of the book, that many organizations do not have a single arts administrator, but a number of people who, though they may carry different titles, effectively carry out the complex practices of arts administration as a team.

Small organizations with one clearly designated administrator do still exist, and some are very successful. In general that would appear to be because, in the case of Matlock's 'First Movement' for example, they are in accord with their overseer constituencies, and have a sharply focused purpose. As First Movement's project co-ordinator, Caroline Bagnall (1993) explains: 'Our specific mission is to ensure that people with profound learning difficulties have the opportunity to be creative. We have developed particularly appropriate and accessible arts events which are tangible, sensory and dynamic.' Where the small organization has a broader and more diffuse purpose – a small arts centre in a small town, for example – the administrator will sometimes find that their power to programme for and shape the image of their centre is very limited indeed. Increasingly, the arts centre's 'mission', and its day-to-day programme, must comply with the funding body's objectives. If the region has, for example, taken an 'initiative' over contemporary dance, the arts centre will be expected to include a proportion of it in their programme, whether there is a local audience for dance or not. The funding body will also insist that all staff and the personnel on the management board meet with their approval. Many of the administrative routines, including all financial returns and applications, must also comply strictly with the overseer body's rules. In all, the administrator of a general arts organization feels increasingly that he or she is a cipher in a 'top down' line management structure.

So this, too, has changed since 1979. Bureaucracy has spread; state funding systems have become more complex, more prescriptive and more intrusive, and arts administration is now more commonly carried on by a team than by an individual. Yet in some respects the essential nature of arts administration has not changed. There is still a wider spread of skills required than for any other profession, except, perhaps, that of career politician, which, interestingly, arts administration most nearly resembles in character (Pick, 1990). The managerial style of arts administration is still characterized by fragmentation, brevity and variety (Mintzberg, 1973). It is still a closed world, with little successful transference of managerial skill from service or manufacturing industry, and indeed little transference from other segments of the leisure industry. Good arts administration is still presumed to depend, to an unusual degree, on 'contacts', and accumulated experience (real and vicarious) of the intricacies of the known 'arts world' (King, 1990).

We have already described in some detail the ways in which arts administration is now changing, and have laid some stress upon the dangers of a swelling bureaucracy, and of allowing the arts to be led, not by artists, nor by their audiences, but by prescriptive planners. To this joint threat – that national 'provision' of culture will become a series of bureaucratically-planned programmes of politically correct 'art', with no heed taken either of the quirky artist or of the reactions of the audience – we must now repeat another. Arts administration and arts provision face the risk of standardization.

More than twenty years ago a cynical observer of state funding for the arts raised the spectre of Britain being full of culture houses '... all ten miles from each other, and all exactly the same' (Herbert, 1957). The threat now is worse. It is that identical culture houses will be filled with identical bureaucrats, all assessed on standard scales, and working in standardized organizations. The Department of National Heritage (1994) announced that a number of large institutions, among them the British Library in London and the National Museums and Galleries on Merseyside, were in the following year to be subjected to financial management and policy reviews (FMPR). The British Quality Assurance Leisure Services Committee (1993), looking to smaller organizations, pronounced its willingness to ensure that 'standards' were everywhere maintained by continuous assessment:

> The introduction of compulsory competitive tendering for local authority services has prompted a growing interest in the subject of Quality Assurance by both the local authorities as clients and those in the public

and private sectors who wish to compete for the opportunity to provide these services. Whilst many managers have prided themselves on the quality of service they provide, the need to ensure that competitive tendering does not lead to a lowering of standards and that value for money is achieved, has led to a new focus on the quality of the service provided and the quality of the management responsible for its delivery.

Meanwhile the Institute of Leisure and Amenity Management (1993), urging the adoption of National Vocational Qualifications throughout the 'leisure industry' suggested that pay could now be related to 'performance':

> Certainly, there is a measure of output often associated with input, like time spent and money invested. It is a close relation of productivity;

that is,
$$\frac{\text{output}}{\text{input}}$$

> But, service is more subtle and should take into account aspects of achievements like on-time delivery, customers' satisfaction, teamworking, accident prevention and quality of service.

All of these moves towards 'maintaining standards' equally involved standardizing management. The presumption is that 'quality of service' in a public art gallery can be measured along the same scale as service in a children's play centre, a computer game station or dance festival. Equally, the presumption is that 'standards' in the theatre, for example, can be monitored in the same way as standards in a hotel or restaurant. Finally, there is the assurance that the 'quality of the management' responsible for the 'delivery' of arts activities as varied as public libraries, brass band festivals, water colourists groups and reminiscence drama can also be ticked off on the same calibrated scale, with marks for 'on-time delivery', 'accident prevention' and of course 'customer satisfaction'.

We cannot emphasise too strongly that such measures are peripheral to the success or otherwise of an arts organization. Overwhelmingly, the most important consideration is the quality of the art. A high degree of customer satisfaction, a lack of accidents, faultless manners of the house staff and the curtain going up on time still do not, in themselves, make a play by Jeffrey Archer a good play, or a Barry Manilow concert a fine musical experience. Next most important is the quality of what we have throughout termed the aesthetic contract: the degree to which a 'proper' audience has been found, and the degree and depth to which the art engages with it. For any arts administrator (or arts administration team) such questions must transcend other important, but more marginal, matters such as punctuality and foyer service.

The different contexts in which arts administrators work, the very different art forms and their different purposes should mean that arts ventures become increasingly dissimilar, not increasingly like each other. We should not worry when, as was anxiously observed in a national study of the public library service in Britain (Worpole, 1991), 'the quality of the service differs from one county or borough to another'. We should be pleased, for, in spite of all the media pressures, and despite the pressures towards managerial conformity, each county and borough has a different character, different needs and a different culture.

9.1 TEAM MANAGEMENT

Researchers have observed that the practice and unitary-oriented arts administrator (see pp.34–35) is often attracted to the 'kind of people' who work in an organization; moreover, groups of people not infrequently leave a job together, and, if they have enjoyed working with each other, later regroup in quite another work setting. Plainly, in normative organizations like arts ventures, 'team spirit' is important, although it is not the unifying gung-ho togetherness which Western commentators sometimes allege is the main characteristic of Japanese factory management, nor the highly focused 'through thick and thin' support which players of team sports are supposed to give each other. It is a more complex, multi-layered series of role-playing interactions which vary in their nature according to daily circumstances.

As the manager works within his organization – characteristically attending short formal meetings, setting goals to small groups, and holding rapidly-convened informal meetings about particular problems with others – he or she will be keenly aware that, for different purposes, different teams suggest themselves as being likely to work well together. It will not necessarily be a matter of whether they are friends, but of whether their personalities interact well, and whether their skills complement each other. It will be clear that for one purpose a team of A, B, C and D would produce results, but, for another question requiring less urgent, more mellow consideration, then B, E and F would be the right grouping.

A day within an arts organization seems to the observer to comprise a lattice of formal and informal meetings. When things are going well the manager will be seen to be subtly co-ordinating them ('co-ordinator' is a much more popular title for arts projects, festivals and educational arts ventures than 'administrator'). When things are going badly there will be a series of informal meetings convened in the corridors, behind office doors or in a nearby pub, without the manager's knowledge, which may – if communications and group solidarity are near breakdown – culminate in a confrontational formal meeting.

The ability to co-ordinate the work of successful arts administration teams depends upon knowing several things about each member of the staff, including their work orientation, experience, knowledge, willingness to cooperate, 'thresholds' of tolerable noise and space in their working environment, time management and current workload. More subtly, it is important to have some knowledge of their opinion of their colleagues, and of their sense of status within the organization.

More important, perhaps, than any of these is the role that they adopt in meetings. This may be quite different from a person's normal character. The extrovert may be clumsily tongue-tied in formal meetings, unable to manipulate a structured gathering. Conversely a quiet and rather grey personality may flower within the safe confines of a formal committee. Equally, some people may be unpredictable, passionate and argumentative when they believe in a cause, and bored and uncooperative when they do not.

A well-known work on the composition of good management teams is that of Belbin (1981). Observing the role-play over twelve years of managers attending the Henley Management School, he eventually proposed eight interactive roles which, he showed, had to be played if any team, board or committee was to work effectively together. He described the roles as follows:

- **The 'Chair'** is the central figure who clarifies objectives, assesses priorities, sets the agendas for meetings, and forms groups and sub-groups to deal with all items. This central figure should be stable, dominant and extrovert.
- **The Company Worker** is characteristically stable and controlled; a practical organizer, who constantly strives for stable structures in which to work. The Company Worker will always try to convert plans into a feasible form, but will sometimes flounder in unstable, quickly-changing conditions.
- **The Resource Investigator** goes outside the group to bring information, ideas and developments back to it. Dominant, stable, extrovert, the Resource Investigator has many outside contacts, and is heavily reliant on them for 'new ideas'.
- **The Monitor Evaluator** characteristically has a high IQ, and is usually introverted by nature. By temperament he or she is likely to be quiet, serious and unemotional, slow to decide anything, and insistent on being in full possession of all the facts before doing so. Most likely to stop colleagues from committing themselves to rash or impulsive action.
- **The Plant** is the grit in the oyster; contrary, given to lateral thinking, impulsive, the Plant is the source of many original ideas, suggestions and proposals. Usually possessing a very high IQ, dominant, erratic and highly prized by colleagues.
- **The Shaper** is anxious and extrovert, usually understood to be the 'task leader' of the group, full of nervous energy, volunteering to take the lead in organizing every project, but tending also to be paranoic. Often has a short fuse, and is easily bored by inaction.
- **The Team Worker** is often the most sensitive of the team, low in dominance, but perceiving and worried by the 'undercurrents' in the team, and the team members' private lives. Gains comfort and assurance from the success of the team and will work hard to hold it together; of great value when there are personality clashes to be resolved.
- **The Finisher** has a vital role. The Finisher is worried about what might go wrong, never at ease until every detail has been personally checked, and sure

that nothing has been overlooked. Hates loose ends, and tends to be intolerant of more slap-happy colleagues. Contributions to discussions tend to be more in the form of questions than statements.

There have of course been many other analysts of team management who have given different titles to these roles, but all analysts seem to be agreed that to work effectively a team needs complementary roles to be played by its members. The authors have had experience both of arts groups that have blown apart because of there being too many wayward 'Plants' clashing, and of committees which have never decided anything, because they comprise a preponderance of good 'Team Workers', with too few 'Resource Investigators' or 'Shapers'. Everyone has probably had experience of boards which have cheerfully driven into disaster because they contained no 'Finishers' in their ranks; the authors recall the board of a South Yorkshire theatre that had no such 'Finisher' and held several monthly meetings before suddenly realizing that the lottery director whom they had appointed at the beginning of the year, far from producing the regular income they had been entering on their monthly accounts, had disappeared to sunnier climes. Nobody had asked the awkward questions; the accumulated debt was more than £100 000; the theatre nearly closed, and the board, rightly, was sacked.

It is important to say in conclusion that Dr Belbin's work does not suggest that there should be eight people at each successful meeting, merely that over time these eight roles have to be played. In the same meeting one person may play two or more roles, or, for different purposes, meeting roles may be reversed. The lesson to be learned is that, in whatever terms, close attention should be given to the team dynamics. As we have been suggesting throughout, such a flexible form has greater leverage towards success in arts organizations than over-standardized 'assessments', or 'performance-related' inducements.

Equally, it is important to remember that building a successful team dynamic does not depend solely upon making the right appointments. It also depends upon the fostering of a clear sense of identity and purpose, upon the speedy and open flow of information within the organization and upon the adoption of what we have come to call holistic arts management.

9.2 HOLISTIC ARTS MANAGEMENT

Many of the pressures from external constituencies tend to break up the homogeneousness of arts organizations. Funding bodies tend increasingly to set extrinsic goals which may strengthen staff commitment to general causes, but lessen commitment to the organization. Such bodies, too, tend to be disruptive of team spirit by insisting on their representation on management boards. As Quine (1991) rightly said:

The pressures of finding the right approach to real strategic planning (not just the Three Year Plan that our funding agencies want); of dealing with greater financial crises; of surviving the present as well as making something of the future; of engaging with the policies of external funding bodies; and of finding time and the constant energy to look for other sources of income: these are all things that a good Board can help with. They are things that a poor Board gets in the way of.

The complexity of the funding bureaucracy also tends to destroy group enthusiasms by involving a great deal of work which shows no tangible results – many applications for sponsorship may have to be made, for example, before there is any response. Overseer and external constituencies consistently make conflicting demands upon the organization, so that it is all too easy to lose a sense of purpose in a chameleon posture which tries to be all things to all people.

The demands of external funding agencies, with their own specialist officers for various purposes, and their own priorities, tend also to mean that the staff of large- and medium-scale arts organizations, in particular, will have a number of specialist arts administrators who have one designated administrative function in their title. As we have said earlier, many organizations have a 'fund raising' officer. Others will have a sponsorship manager. Some will have a marketing officer, others someone in charge of mailing, or a sales or subscriptions manager. Some have PR officers. When it was a priority with the Arts Council of Great Britain some arts organizations appointed education officers. Larger bodies have a head of planning. Touring groups often have road managers. Each person is appointed with discrete responsibility for that segment of the organization's work, and usually that person will be responsible for its successful delivery to an external body. Plainly this is not a good recipe for a balanced and homogeneous organization. Indeed it is, potentially, a recipe for bad administration, for the majority of tasks fall between the designated categories, and thus the usual comment made about organizations that are misfiring is that there are 'too many chiefs'. Nobody wants to be involved in the myriad tasks which fall to the ordinary braves and squaws. Yet those tasks constitute the majority of the day-to-day administration, and contribute more to the managerial efficiency of the organization than the completion only of tasks which fall into the designated categories.

Let us take, as examples, two the tasks mentioned above – gaining sponsorship, and PR for the organization. It is fair to say that the success or otherwise of any arts organization may well depend upon the successful accomplishment of the former, and certainly will depend on the successful management of the latter. Thus, even though they may be the prime responsibility of one designated member of staff, everybody should be involved in them. Everyone in the organization should be equipped with material which sets out the organization's aims and all that it offers potential sponsors. Everyone should be ready to bring back their own contacts who may be approached for sponsorship. Everyone (including technicians and performers) must be prepared, when it is appropriate, to approach contacts on the organization's behalf.

Involvement by all staff is even more necessary when we turn to PR, and the organization's 'image'. In 1977 the Institute of Contemporary Arts in London presented a controversial exhibition, 'Pornography', by an artist called Genesis P. Orridge. At its preview the Arts Council officers present made it clear that they disliked it, but, according to the 'arm's length principle' defended the organization's right to show it. All might have been well, had not a tabloid newspaper rung the gallery quite early the following morning. The person who answered was a woman cleaner. When asked what she thought of the exhibition, she replied that she thought it was disgusting. Then, when asked if she was on the staff, she replied truthfully that she was. The following day the newspapers headlined the fact that the ICA staff thought it was disgusting. As a result of the furore that incident caused, the director and several staff members resigned, and the ICA had a period in the doldrums.

The 'image' of an organization is thus not created by a PR specialist, though such a person may put a 'spin' on news stories. Rather, it is formed by the total effect of the way the organization operates, by the sum total of all of the contacts which all members of staff (full- and part-time) have with the general public, and by the impressions carried away with them by the general public. Too often such accumulated contacts and impressions contradict the image promulgated by the publicity material. Organizations which pronounce themselves 'innovative' and 'exciting' are perceived as being fractious and dull. Organizations which describe themselves as purposeful and determined are perceived as sloppy and opinionated.

The authors have, over the past twenty years, worked with arts organizations in more than twenty countries. They have constantly been surprised, when visiting a distant town or city, by how readily ordinary people (taxi drivers, hotel waiters, shopkeepers) will give a confident assessment of the success or failings of the management of a local museum, opera house or arts precinct. Their assessment is often at odds with expensively produced publicity material. They have been told, often quite gratuitously, of internal disagreements, of lack of co-ordination, of waste, incompetence, carelessness with money, rudeness to visitors – all of it in contradiction to the image the arts organization is trying to foster.

Adoption of team administration and holistic management involves recognizing that each decision within an arts organization will tend to reflect on all aspects of the organization's work and will contribute, positively or negatively, to the image of the organization. It also involves recognition of the fact that no administrative decision has its effect only in the present. All decisions have future effects. They must therefore be taken with half an eye on the future. One cannot present a populist programme this season, to make money, so that one can present avant-garde work in the next, for the future audience's expectations will be shaped by the character of this year's shows. And this year's ticket prices will also be shaping expectations for next year. For many years the Royal Shakespeare Company had an unusually high 'top' price for a short period during the height of their Stratford summer season, so that people had seen the high price, and were prepared for it the following year.

There will of course be many entertainment and arts corporations, and many arts bureaucracies, for whom this approach is not appropriate. It is, however, appropriate for those many organizations that are more or less dependent upon external support, but are anxious to retain their own identity with a team committed to their goals.

Holistic management is, then, the opposite of compartmentalized, short-term or 'top down' management. It depends upon the organization having clear and purposeful aims, and upon the adoption of general team management techniques. That, in turn, means that there are no absolute specialists, but that everyone is expected to take some part in matters of general concern, be willing to share tasks which are of general responsibility, and be ready to share information about their own particular concerns. The particular characteristics of holistic arts management are as follows:

- The aims and objectives of the organization are adopted by everyone, and are subjected to periodic review by all staff.
- The programme and other work of the organization is regularly and fully discussed with all staff. So far as possible all staff members are empowered to consider themselves agents of the organization, its programme and its 'image'.
- No information, including planning, administrative and technical information, is kept secret.
- All decisions are made in clearly designated ways by the best groups or teams that can be assembled for the purpose from full- and part-time staff. Each decision is arrived at with as full an understanding as possible of the effect it will have upon every part of the organization.
- So far as is possible, equal status is conferred upon all the different members of the staff. All staff share in successes and all take some blame for failures.
- The staff will together assess their strengths and weaknesses, and individuals will be assessed so far as is possible by their peers.

In suggesting this approach, we are doing no more than saying that arts organizations should draw upon their own traditions. It is that shared sense of purpose that has sustained groups of poets and painters, travelling musicians and bands of strolling players for centuries. Not the least of the aims of modern arts administration must be to bring back into the arts a sense of camaraderie and shared joy.

REFERENCES

Bagnall, C. (1993) 'Changing the Ownership', in *Mailout* (ed M. Schwarz), (Oct/Nov).
Belbin, M. (1981) *Management Teams*.

BQA (1993) *Quality Assurance for Leisure Services.*

Herbert, A.P. (1957) No Fine on Fun; *The Comical History of the Entertainments Duty.*

ILAM (1993) *Performance-Related Pay in the Leisure Industry* (Fact Sheet 93/5).

King, I. (1990) *A Study of Decision-making by Managers in the Popular Theatre.*

Margerison, C. and McCann, D. (1991) *Team Management.*

Mintzberg, H. (1973) *The Nature of Managerial Work.*

Pick, J. (1990) 'Have arts administrators changed their nature?', in *Cultural Management* (ed A. Priestley), Vol. 8, No. 2.

Quine, M. (1991) 'Treading Around the Boards', in *The Stage* (July 11).

Worpole, K. (1991) *Borrowed Time? The Future of Public Libraries in the UK.*

Case studies

The case studies in this section are fictional (though based on common problems faced by real arts administrators) and may be used in a variety of ways. They may be used by the individual reader to sharpen his or her wits, or, perhaps more profitably, they may be used by groups working together, who use the scenarios here as a basis for discussion.

Three things they are not. They are not detailed documentary accounts. In every case the reader will have to make a number of assumptions about further details, and will have to flesh out the given data. (In group discussions, discussions over what would be 'reasonable assumptions' to make about circumstantial detail can be, in the authors' experience, valuable.) Nor are the cases straightforwardly linked to the chapters of the book. It would be a betrayal of all we said in the book's introduction were we now to say that reading the foregoing text has given the reader everything he or she requires to unravel these and other problems. The cases cut across the topics discussed earlier in the book, and draw on the reader's experience outside it. Finally, the case studies do not have one 'correct' answer. Although we have offered a few notes to help work on the cases, we should expect lively minds to disagree with much that we say, and to offer their own answers.

Some other specialist texts would certainly be helpful with particular case studies. In this context we should like to commend Diggle, K. (1994) *Arts Marketing*, Tomlinson, R. (1994) *Boxing Clever: How to Get the Most out of the Box Office*, and Raymond, C. (1993) *Clear Sightlines*.

10.1 GETTING THE TEAM TOGETHER

The members of the newly-created board of the Applewick Arts Centre were well-satisfied with themselves. From the window of their meeting room in a prefabricated building on the corner of the Arts Centre site they could see the construction workers busy on the roof of the new extension being added to the warehouse that they had purchased only three short years ago. An EU development grant, added to the grants they had secured from two national foundations, had provided the bulk of the funds. They had also had some help from their local authority, but the major assistance from the Applewick Council lay in the revenue grant of £75 000 a year which it had pledged to the Arts Centre for the next three years.

Applewick is not well provided for at present. There is a small exhibition space in the local museum, a handsome old Town Hall which is used for concerts and occasional stage shows, a large and well-equipped hall in a comprehensive school on the edge of town which is used by the amateur operatic society, and an old cinema, now divided into three rather small auditoria. Evening classes thrive in the town, and there is a local music club, three amateur drama societies and an art club – but, in general, there is not much professional work seen at present in the town.

After a good deal of debate, it had been decided that the Arts Centre would contain two large exhibition spaces (properly equipped with gallery lighting and screens, three soundproofed workshops, a theatre seating 275 (with dressing-rooms, a well-appointed stage and fully-equipped control box) and a handsome foyer, part of which would be occupied by tables from the cafeteria counter. The two small bars and the cafeteria had been sublet for the first year to a local catering company, for an annual rental of £15 000.

Separate sponsorship had equipped the box office and director's office with computer systems, and local sponsors had given an intercom system, and a good Bechstein grand, to the Arts Centre. In the business plan it was calculated that wages, full- and part-time (including employers' costs), would amount to some £120 000 in the first year. It is anticipated that the Arts Centre will be open seven days a week.

The board has been much heartened by the local support it has received. The town of Applewick contains 50 000 people and there are a further 75 000 people living within a radius of thirty miles. More than 500 of them have been involved in the campaign to open the Arts Centre, and 350 have already joined the 'Friends of Applewick' society. They are happy to help out as gallery stewards, ushers or security, or anything else which is required.

The anticipated opening is only six months away. The board has already advertised for a director ('with experience, flair and imagination') to open the new centre. They expect to pay their new leader some £18 000 a year. Today's meeting however is to draw up a general plan for the staffing of the centre, which will of course be discussed with the new director before any action is taken upon it. There are already signs of some disagreement amongst board members. Some think that there should be assistant directors with responsibility for the visual and the performing arts, while others think that the priority must lie with appointing good support staff – professional box office, marketing, stage and front-of-house staff. Still others think that appointments to the full-time staff should be kept to a minimum, and that as many voluntary and part-time staff as possible should be hired from Applewick.

Given the constraints, what kind of staffing structure would you urge upon the new director?

GROUP WORK In groups of eight to ten people, hold the board discussion, and try to get unanimity for a workable staffing structure.

10.2 CONTRACTING FOR ART

A radical new government has given notice that it intends to change the way government funding is administered. In the Western Region, the 120 arts organizations that receive funding have been told that, at the end of the next financial year, the Western Regional Arts Board, which has dispensed some £8 000 000 to them annually, is to be wound up. In subsequent years the funding body, covering the same area, will be a private organization, Western Cultural Development Plc. This organization has a three-year franchise to supervise the distribution of £10 000 000 annually, with the following strict guidelines:

1. Only 4% of turnover may be spent on administration.
2. All decisions are to be made by boards, chaired by WCD staff, but elected from local arts constituencies. In general, arts development should be in line with national guidelines.
3. All contracts with clients are to be in a format acceptable to the National Ministry, and open to continuous inspection.
4. WCD is to consider itself accountable both to government, and to the local community. It will be expected therefore to publish regular reports, hear representations from the community, and have regular general meetings.
5. WCD may engage in any legal practice to add to its government funding allocation, but may not use government funds for any purpose other than arts promotion, and grant aid.
6. It will be expected to balance its budget at the end of the franchise.
7. No company owned or partly owned by WCD, nor any member of WCD staff may benefit in any way from the funding administered during this period.
8. Government will pay an annual fee to WCD on the satisfactory completion of each year.

Western Arts Board at present covers an area which contains twenty-six local authorities and a total population of 4 000 000. In broad terms, its 120 clients are funded as follows:

Table 10.1 Funding of WAB clients

| | Funding from each source | | |
	Western Arts Board	Local Authority	Sponsorship
Drama venues (11)	45%	15%	5%
Visual Arts (16)	70%	25%	2%
Drama touring (3)	35%	20%	1%
Music (30)	50%	10%	6%
Community Arts (20)	30%	25%	10%
Film and Video (15)	50%	10%	—
Festivals (10)	30%	30%	5%
Incoming tours (15)	35%	15%	15%

The amounts of money allocated to each area were broadly as follows:

	£
Drama venues	210 000
Visual Arts	1 280 000
Drama touring	940 000
Music	1 100 000
Community Arts	925 000
Film and Video	875 000
Festivals	1 220 000
Incoming Tours	650 000

The remainder was spent on administration.

Additionally, it should be noted that the local government authorities fund an additional 240 groups not in receipt of funding from Western Arts Board. These include several literary groups and a number of amateur societies. These additional funds total £1 250 000. Tourism attracts a further 2 500 000 visitors to the area, and the top ten tourist attractions in the region (theme parks, historic sites, and a large zoo) have a combined turnover of £12 000 000.

The working party of Western Cultural Development is now about to start its first meeting. There has been general dissatisfaction over Western Arts Board's laborious system of deficit funding, and, now freed of administrative shackles (WCD have been told they may make awards to non-charities, and may adopt any accountable system to fund their clients), the WCD Working Party is sitting down to decide what system it is going to adopt. Not unnaturally, the arts organizations (and the local authorities) are agog to learn what systems will be discussed and then adopted.

Consider new and better ways of funding arts organizations in the West, and list the realistic options faced by WCD. Suggest how each option might be met within the budget.

GROUP WORK In small groups decide both how the budget is to be allocated by WCD, and together decide on three possible ways of funding clients in future.

10.3 WORKING WITH THE SYSTEM

Three friends from college days meet each Friday night for a drink. They are all working, but none of them is doing something which really interests them. (Their interests range from rock music to the cultivation of rare orchids.) They used to joke about one day running their own company, and now it seems it could come true.

One night the three unexpectedly bump into an older and eccentric friend, famous locally for running a lively local night-club, and a weekly magazine for young people, both named *After Dark*. He tells them that he has had a religious experience, and is going to give up both of his businesses and retire to a life of devout meditation on a remote Scottish island. They tell him enviously that they cannot afford to take risks like that.

To their surprise he then offers both of his businesses to the young trio, for the price of a local semi-detached house. He tells them they could easily borrow the money from a bank, as the businesses are both highly profitable, and would easily repay the interest, as well as providing a reasonable income for the trio. When they say that they know nothing about either business he tells them that both have competent managers, and that they 'run themselves'.

The night-club is open every evening except Sunday and Monday. It offers food, drinks, a dance floor and, on Fridays and Saturdays, a live midnight 'cabaret'. The manager is careful to ensure the music follows the latest trends. It has a full-time staff of five (including a bouncer with proper NVQs), and a dozen or so part-time staff. It is run in full cooperation with the local police, and there seems to be no reason why it should not continue profitably for several years.

The magazine took nearly a year to establish itself, but it now regularly sells 25 000 copies. It has recently run articles on jazz in Hamburg, the soul scene in Carolina, rap poetry in Britain, hip hop in Amsterdam. There are excellently photographed fashion pages, an agony uncle, sections on Where To Hang Out, the latest video releases, hair grooming – and occasional 'way out' pieces such as The World of Ice Cream, the Window Box Garden, Cycling, and Religions of the New Age. It has a full-time staff of three (who feel overworked and suggest they need two extra full-time members of staff) and a range of freelance writers and photographers who are paid for items they contribute. It has now been steadily profitable for eighteen months.

What advice would you give to the trio?

GROUP WORK Working as either the full-time staff of the night-club, or the full-time staff of the magazine, prepare a presentation to the three potential buyers, saying what needs to be done to ensure continued success.

10.4 CREATING A FESTIVAL

In five year's time Duncastle, a pleasant but unremarkable market town with 45 000 inhabitants, will celebrate the 700th anniversary of the granting of its charter. The town has decided to celebrate this in a big way with a festival. (The anniversary date is 10 June.)

Two arenas are being renovated, on money acquired partly through local subscription and partly through a National Lottery award. The first is Duncastle Park – rambling parkland of some 150 acres, given to the town by a local landowner 100 years ago. In the park a new open-air auditorium is being created, capable of accommodating 1600 people, by the side of the lake. There is also to be a newly created sculpture park and, by the well-screened new car parks, a new adventure playground for children. All this work will be complete four years from now.

The second arena is a remarkable Edwardian concert hall known locally as the Market Hall, for in recent years it has been used largely as a covered market. This is being renovated and refurbished. It will seat 690 people, facing a capacious stage which is capable of accommodating a full orchestra. Not the least of the Market Hall's attractions is that it has three large and pleasant reception rooms on the first floor. The entrance is just off the market place, right in the middle of the town.

Duncastle still boasts a railway station, and a major motorway runs nearby. There are thirty-two restaurants listed in the town, and at present a total of 220 beds in local hotels and guest-houses. There is one multiplex cinema, a town hall with a proscenium stage, and the Carrivale Art Gallery, a part of the library building. Amateur art is strong in the area; the local amateur drama groups have created their own theatre in a disused chapel on the edge of the town (where the six local dancing schools hold their annual shows); the three local choirs give their concerts in the splendid old parish church, St Nicholas at Duncastle.

A group of local citizens has been elected, at a public meeting, to form a working party to plan the festival. The regional arts council and the local authority have already signalled their interest in helping, and already two local industrialists have mentioned that they expect to be approached for sponsorship moneys.

The working party now meets. It has only hazy notions of the form the festival may take, but the members know that some things (applying for grant aid, or booking some artistes) need to be considered a long way ahead. Some of the working party have recently attended a course on holistic management, and know that the festival needs to be broadly conceived in its entirety before anything is planned in detail, or any public announcements are made.

Create an exciting programme for the festival, and draw up a flow chart which suggests when applications for grant aid and for licensing must be made, when artists must be booked, when such matters as accommodation, parking and transport must be dealt with, and which also sets out a broad marketing strategy.

GROUP WORK In groups create an exciting programme for the festival, and draw up a strategy for working with the tourist authorities to draw 3000 people a day into Duncastle for the duration of the festival.

10.5 BALANCING THE BUDGET

Massive support from Europe, the Millennium Fund, and the large Metropolitan authority of Sudfield was instrumental in setting up a splendid new media centre in a former secondary school building near the centre of the city. It was handsomely equipped, and set up to run with a full-time staff of nine, four of whom were expert technicians, two administering the programme in the auditoria, the three others forming the administrative team. Twelve part-timers were regularly employed throughout the year. Catering was a self-contained operation, designed to be profitable, and cleaning was franchised to a private company from the city.

In its first year the Sudfield Media Centre was free of financial worry. It was supported by revenue grants of £65 000 from the Regional Arts Board and £45 000 from the local authority. It attracted £130 000 in sponsorship, and had a BFI grant of £80 000. Its facilities were new, and attractive. The three film-making studios were in almost continuous use (they cost only £30 an hour to hire, with the use of a skilled technician) and such facilities as the two editing suites and the six darkrooms were also popular. The two small recording studios were also much used, and, partly because of additional local sponsorship of £15 000, they were able to offer the opportunity for local groups to make tapes and discs for less than £100. Most successful of all were the two auditoria, which seat 400 and 150 people respectively. On average there were showings on four nights a week in both. Attendances averaged some 50% over the year in the larger auditoria, and 60% in the smaller one. Admission averaged £3 for a single admittance, but a season ticket, which admitted the bearer to any showing throughout the year, was only £75. That proved popular, and there were 200 season tickets sold last year.

In all, receipts from the general public totalled £85 000, although the cafeteria by the main entrance (which is set up as a separate trading company and employs its own staff) made a slight loss. Expenditure in the first financial year was as follows.

		£
Salaries	full-time	180 000
	part-time	65 000
Repair and maintenance		35 000
Security		25 000
Insurance		8 000
Contracted cleaning		45 000
Materials		58 000
Loss on cafeteria		4 000

Next year does not, however, look so good. The cost of materials is expected to rise by 10% overall, and a fault has been discovered in the air duct and central heating system, so the costs of repair and maintenance will rise to £70 000. All wages and salaries will rise by 5%.

More serious is the fact that the revenue grant from the local authority looks as if it will have to be cut by 15%, the special local sponsorship of the recording studios is not going to be repeated, and in spite of all the staff efforts it seems as if sponsorship in general will total no more than £110 000. Other support is holding steady, but plainly the second year of operation looks as if it is going to make a serious loss.

You are asked to give advice on reorganizing the programme so that the centre works within budget. Make a list of all the additional information you will need to have before you can do this, and then make a series of recommendations.

GROUP WORK The administrative team invite the technical staff to join them for a crisis meeting, and draw up a workable budget for the second year of operation. This will involve a new programme, with a new scale of charges, and a somewhat different 'image'.

10.6 MARKETING THE ARTS

The Varsity Magic Opera Company is to play ten autumn dates, playing on average for four nights in each venue. Their programme is not continuous, and there are breaks between performances, sometimes for several days. They have three productions in their repertoire – a surreal production of *The Magic Flute*, a resurrected success of four years ago, called *Post Coital*, which has a rock score, and a new work, specially written for them, based on the life of Virginia Woolf, called *Make Waves!*. The same small orchestra plays for all three pieces. Usually, the singers play in at least two, sometimes all three, of the operas that are toured. The company has a reasonable reputation, and (assisted by subsidy) can usually balance the books doing a 70/30 split with the theatres they visit. (That is, the visiting company takes 70% of the box office receipts.)

Normally things work smoothly. The theatres which book the company choose which performances they would like from the repertoire, and then the Varsity Magic Opera Company sends them posters, fly sheets, photographs and other advertising material several weeks in advance. At many dates they are 'pencilled in' each year, without the VMOC marketing director having to work too hard to get bookings.

This year, however, it has been different. First, times are hard for the theatres, so many of them have been trying to renegotiate the 70/30 split. Worse, there has been a big imbalance in the bookings of shows. *The Magic Flute* has been requested 28 times, *Post Coital* 10 and *Make Waves!* only twice. Even that would be bearable but the Virginia Woolf piece has a bravura soprano part, and the company has slightly overextended its budget by booking Virginia Lucas. Ms Lucas is of course very expensive, and has insisted on a contract paying her the normal high fee for the whole autumn season, irrespective of how frequently she is called upon to perform the role in public. As things stand, the receipts from two performances will not pay the set designer's fee, let alone the soprano's!

There are six weeks to go before the tour begins, and rehearsals, costume-making and set building are getting under way. The theatre managers who have booked the programme refuse to alter their choices, and Virginia Lucas refuses to have her contract changed (though she is perfectly happy to play more performances, if any are arranged). Then, after a series of stormy meetings, the marketing director resigns, claiming that his task is impossible. Bad feeling starts to grow in the company, and rumours begin to circulate suggesting that the VMOC will go bankrupt before the tour is over. Then two of the theatre managers who have booked the tour ring up to say that they have heard disquieting rumours, and ask pointedly whether the tour is still on ...

What should be done to resurrect the company's image, to reshape the tour and to market it successfully?

GROUP WORK An emergency meeting of the Opera Company's management board considers what must be done about replacing the marketing director, making the tour financially viable and restoring the company's former reputation.

10.7 BUILDING THE AUDIENCE

The Bruddersford Civic Theatre (which seats 700 people) has, after twenty years of serving Bruddersford and district (population 100 000) under the direct control of council officers, been contracted out to the newly formed Libra Theatre Company. Bruddersford is a solid northern community, and the decision was not taken lightly.

The terms of the contract are that responsibility for maintenance and repair remains with the council, and that the council makes no charge for the furnishings and fittings of the theatre (including all box office systems and stage equipment) which are leased to Libra on a two-year contract. The council will continue to pay for an external cleaning service. Under the terms of the contract Libra will be responsible for replacement parts of all technical equipment.

For many years the district council has run the theatre with the same sort of programme, a few short runs of popular touring plays, a few amateur productions (for which the theatre has hitherto been 'let' at a low fee), a three-week Christmas pantomime, and a large number of one-night stands – comedians, singers, pop groups and appearances by 'celebrities'. The programme has been advertised in a regular, if uninspired, way, with hanging cards, mailshots of the programme leaflet, newspaper advertising and a colourful photographic display in the front of the theatre. The prices have been kept fairly low, with generous concession rates, but there have been no attempts at subscription selling, and only cursory attempts to draw in party bookings.

Audiences have been dwindling, and in the last year the total box office 'take' fell by 15%. Attendances overall in the theatre were around 45%. A commissioned survey suggested that many Bruddersford people preferred to go to the theatres in nearby large cities, because it was 'more exciting'. The respondents found the foyers, bars and restaurant at the theatre (all of which have been in the control of the council) adequate, but also unexciting. As a result the district council decided to contract out the running of the theatre. Libra, who gained the contract, is to be paid £125 000 a year to run the theatre 'with a mixed programme to appeal to all sectors'. The council has also offered the complete bar and catering franchise to Libra, but require £25 000 payment for this. (If Libra do not take up this offer the council will offer it elsewhere.)

The Libra directors will have to move quickly. They have three months to fashion the winter programme (only a few one-night stands by well-known 'stars' have been firmly booked so far). More importantly, they have to create the outlines of a wholly new marketing strategy.

The directors are well aware that the two tasks are inseparable, but that neither is easy. Bruddersford is a deeply conservative place. Evenings out for the locals seem to be set in predictable ruts, and though tourists often stay in Bruddersford (there are three excellent old hotels, with a total of 107 bedrooms) they then go on to spend the day in nearby National Trust properties, and in visiting distant cathedrals. A new, vivid and effective marketing strategy will not be easy to create.

Devise a programme which you feel would, with good publicity and promotion, appeal to all sectors of the Bruddersford community, and then devise a good marketing programme for it.

GROUP WORK The Bruddersford Leisure and Recreation Committee meets to decide on the criteria by which the success or otherwise of the Libra management is to be judged.

10.8 THE AMATEUR SOCIETIES

Sherton (population 200 000) has always prided itself on its traditions in music. Visits by touring opera companies to the Grand Opera House (capacity 950) are always well supported. The annual Festival of Orchestral Music can claim an international reputation, and there are thriving choral societies, brass bands and lovers of organ music. The choir in St Winifred's, the largest church, is still well worth hearing. However, in two areas of local musical life, there are problems.

a) The amateur operatic society

The Sherton Operatic and Dramatic Society celebrated its sixtieth anniversary last year, with a production of *Oklahoma*, which ran for a week at the Grand Opera House. Unfortunately, it lost money. The production costs (including hire of scenery and costumes, and paying musicians' union rates to the orchestra) exceeded £16 000. Worse, the payment to the management of the Grand (a hiring fee of £8000, plus management fees which had VAT added) totalled £11 000. They had calculated that, with full houses for all six performances and an average seat price of £6, they would break even. Unfortunately, they did not fill every performance and lost £3000.

The society dipped heavily into reserves to wipe off that deficit, but now it faces the problem of the next production. Next time the total costs of using the Grand Theatre are likely to be around £12 000. They wish to perform *Kismet*, for which they estimate the production costs will again total £16 000.

Some members of the society, however, argue that it would be far more sensible to use the Corn Exchange Hall which though smaller (capacity 450) is far cheaper. This costs only £3000 to hire for the week. Its two disadvantages, apart from lower capacity, are that the society has to stage-manage the show and that there is no orchestra pit, merely floor-level space for the musicians. Others in the society argue that this is quite the wrong way of looking at the problem, and that the society should continue to use the Grand Theatre (whose management has always been very cooperative), endeavouring to find local sponsors who would make good the inevitable 'loss'.

List arguments for and against using each venue, and offer any other solution you can see to the society's problem.

GROUP WORK The operatic society committee meets to thrash out the problem, having nominated two people to summarize the arguments for the Grand and the arguments for using the Corn Exchange.

b) The music society

The Sherton Music Society also has a long history. It presents, every year, one recital a month between September and March by visiting professional artists, in the Corn Exchange Hall. For the last four years both membership and public attendances have steadily declined. Yet in two years' time the society wishes to mark its fiftieth year with a celebratory season.

Acting on advice the committee has hired a local consultant to advise it both on how to reverse the decline, and how to hold its fiftieth anniversary celebrations successfully. For a small fee, the consultant agrees to present a diagnostic report only.

This the consultant does. The problem, the committee is informed, is that they are stuck in a rut. They have an ageing membership, a moribund committee, and a silly pricing system which allows members to attend cheaply on a membership fee which is rarely raised, and forces visitors to pay more than twice as much. Worst of all, the annual programme is utterly predictable. It always consists of one each of: piano solo; solo voice and piano; string quartet; wind or brass quintet; solo violin and piano; other solo instrument and piano. Apart from anything else, the consultant says, this raises costs because of the high cost of hiring a good piano for so many of the concerts.

What is needed, the consultant says, is a strategy for the next three years, to broaden the programme and attract new and larger audiences. Moreover, the strategy must not be based on the premise that the society's only income is from ticket sales for its concert series; there are many people in the society well used to fundraising, and many have leisure time. Members must work for their music, and not just sit back and enjoy it!

Prepare a programme of both musical events and allied fund raising activities which enable the society to celebrate its anniversary in style.

GROUP WORK Working parties are formed of music group members, one to consider a three-year programme of fund raising activities, another the three-year development of the concert programme. The two committees present their results to each other and decide on ways in which the two activities can complement each other.

10.9 THE THREAT OF THE MULTIPLEX

Six months ago Georgina Emgea spent nearly all the money her parents had left her in purchasing a 400-seater single screen cinema (built originally as a theatre) which was only just making a profit. She took over as manager. The cinema has a projectionist (who is also the assistant manager), two part-time receptionists (usherettes) and one part-time box office assistant. Cleaning and maintenance have both, so far, been done by Georgina and her assistant.

In the six months she has learned how to project a film; she has also worked in the box office, and taken out the tray sales in the intervals. She has not changed the pattern of the programme much. Mostly she shows the same film for a week (though sometimes she has to show a film for longer if she is to have it at all), one evening performance daily. At school holidays, including half terms, she shows a U, PG or 12 certificated film daily at 6 p.m. (plus matinée on Saturdays), followed by a 15 or 18 film at 8 p.m. Particularly in those periods, pre-performance and confectionary sales are good, and at the end of the first six months Georgina has not only paid herself a modest wage, but the private cinema has also made a slight profit.

Things look rosy. There is only one other cinema in the large town in which she operates, and her customers tell her that they prefer coming to her cinema partly because it has 'a bit of character', but also because it has a large, well-lit car park and is near bus stops for the town's major routes.

Then comes the bombshell. She hears that in four months' time a major entertainment corporation is opening a large multiplex cinema on the outskirts of the town. Her first reaction is that her enterprise is doomed.

Advise the cinema owner on a strategy for survival.

GROUP WORK The entertainment corporation is applying for planning permission to erect the multiplex. The cinema manager, her assistant and owners of other entertainments in the town – the three night-clubs, the tenpin bowling, some of the larger pubs – meet to discuss whether they should adopt a common strategy in the face of this news.

10.10 HAVING A GOOD DAY

The Castle Wyndham Hotel and Crafts Centre is a well-established attraction in the South. The hotel, pleasantly built just below the jagged skyline of the old castle, has 32 bedrooms and can accommodate upwards of 60 people. Many of the residents come on the fairly expensive, but worthwhile courses run in the crafts centre.

The centre is built around the old castle well, and comprises six well-equipped workshops, two kilns, a smithy and darkrooms for photography. Nearer to the large car park there is the visitors' centre with the handsome Bridle Path Gallery, restaurant and several crafts shops. On average 350 people a day visit the crafts centre.

The hotel and crafts centre is owned and operated by a private company, Wyndham Enterprise plc. They employ a managing director, who is responsible to the board for the whole concern. Responsible in turn to the managing director are the hotel manager, a crafts centre manager and a head of crafts education. In addition there are sixteen other full-time, and twenty-six part-time staff. Although the complex is less profitable than it was, it is holding its own (the average hotel occupancy is 55%, the twenty-four crafts courses held this year are all fully subscribed, and the average 'spend' of each visitor to the crafts centre is £4.50). The whole complex has recently been expensively refurbished (which supposedly cost Wyndham Enterprises £750 000) and there are hopes that this will attract even more business.

The managing director was working eighteen hours a day, right up to the moment when the airport taxi came, but the three weeks' holiday has been a tonic. However, as soon as he or she walks back into the office, anxiety returns. These are the first messages to be seen:

1. Emergency meeting of the board of Wyndham Enterprises at 11 o' clock that morning. (No agenda available.)
2. Confidential note saying that the crafts centre manager has offered to resign. (No explanation offered, but one will be given 'when they talk'.)
3. Message from receptionist asking the managing director to phone the local police station, and also to phone the public liability insurers, as soon as possible.
4. A letter of complaint from a Mr and Mrs Foljambe, who recently came on a woodcarving course, and who claim the tutor was rude to them, and that the facilities were inadequate.
5. A telephone message to say that the managing director's secretary is ill and won't be able to come in that day.
6. Fax from Sir Humphrey, chairman of the board, asking whether the managing director has yet heard from Mr and Mrs Foljambe, who are 'good friends of mine'.
7. A second fax, from Rodney Clinker, the editor of the local newspaper,

saying that they won't go to print with the story of 'events at Wyndham' until the managing director has had a talk with him. However they have to meet the printers' deadline at 10 o' clock that morning.

It is now a quarter to nine. As the managing director digests these alarming messages, there is a knock on the door of the office. ...

Advise the managing director. What are the priorities, and how can a prudent path be steered through the next three hours?

GROUP WORK The members of the management board meet, having all had slightly different information on the 'events' of the previous days. They then ask the managing director to leave the room, and decide what courses of action to take.

POINTS TOWARDS ANSWERS

10.1 Getting the team together

There is much to be said for not creating too rigid a structure. It would be better if, before the director arrives on the scene, lists were to be made of the specialized skills and knowledge required by some staff, the technical and operating skills required by some staff, and the kinds of qualities required by **all** staff. Advertisements could then invite applications from people whose experience and skills fitted some, if not all, of the criteria. It would certainly be good if the director could be closely involved in making the first appointment, and then the appointing body were gradually widened to include new appointees – so that, ideally, the last member to be appointed would be selected by the whole of the rest of the team. Such a 'dynamic' route, however, demands that each member of staff be carefully contracted to work with colleagues in certain agreed areas, and equally demands that each appointee is contracted to undertake a certain number of general duties. When this is not done, demarcation disputes, and squabbles over the 'prestige' of certain tasks, are both common.

10.2 Contracting for art

Plainly this is an opportunity to think carefully about the alternatives to 'deficit funding'. Three possibilities are:

- **Contract funding** Artists and organizations could effectively be 'commissioned' for short, medium and long periods to provide the public with art. The money could be, in part, paid 'up front' on condition that the funded person or organization meets stipulated requirements.
- **Awards** Certain sums of money are offered for competitive tender, a suitable panel or committee choosing the 'winner' in each case.
- **Endowments** These involve depositing a certain sum of money, the interest on which pays for a specified cause. There is no reason why the new organization could not combine these. It may also enlarge its own income by gaining sponsorship, or by offering its own franchise on certain services and profit-making opportunities in the arts throughout the region.

10.3 Working with the system

Two things seem to be evident. The motives of the generous friend may not be unmixed, and, even if he is as generous as he appears, the *After Dark* night club would be interfered with at the trio's peril. It would be better to concentrate on the magazine, noting that similar magazines are increasingly tied up with merchandising deals (i.e. they 'give away' compact discs, or make fabulous 'free offers' to their readers in association with various manufacturers, whose continued advertising support is essential to the magazine's economy). It would be essential to explore the economics of magazine publication in some detail. Essential, too, to find out something of the ways in which such a magazine keeps its fingers on the 'pulse' of its readership. The staff may be asking for more help because they know that they no longer feel this pulse.

10.4 Creating a festival

The first thing a working party would have to do is to look at all the other festivals planned for that time, in that area. The Duncastle Festival must have a 'unique selling proposition' at the core. This is doubly effective if it could be tied in with a local historical character or event, so that it is, for example, the 'Samuel Bickerstaff Ballooning and Brass Band Festival'. From the start, the event will need an 'image' – including logo, advertising slogans and promotional stunts. All these are much easier to create if the working party were to start by imagining a successful festival. It is sometimes best for the group to 'talk through' an ideal event, describing the artistes and the crowds, and what they are doing. Then the elements in the marketing mix tend more readily to take shape.

10.5 Balancing the budget

The commonest mistake in such a situation is to begin by making economies. The organization which does this – closing one day a week, opening the box office for fewer hours, trying to make two part-timers do a full-timer's work – frequently finds itself in a descending economic spiral. The economies mean less money is taken, so next time further economies have to be made.

The centre seems to have undercharged badly in its first year, and must now increase charges to a viable level. This cannot however be achieved abruptly. It is much better to introduce sliding scales of charges, even charges which are seasonally adjusted, or alternatively to raise prices generally but introduce a wide range of concessions. There must be close examination, too, of whether additional charges should not be made for some materials.

Plainly the cafeteria needs drastic reorganization, but there is reason to be cautious about increasing the season ticket charge. More needs to be known about the users. It may be that the attractively-priced season ticket draws to the centre many people who spend money using it in other ways, so an increase in season ticket prices would have an adverse effect throughout the centre.

10.6 Marketing the arts

The late marketing director is, in one way, no loss. He was hysterically wrong about the economics of the autumn season. It is always a mistake to budget separately for each production, as it is for each show in a venue. It is the overall budget that matters. Here it is likely that the 'profits' on *The Magic Flute* and *Post Coital* will more than 'pay' for *Make Waves!*. The company can in any case promote other performances of the new opera in venues booked to fill the present breaks in the tour. Consideration should be given to presenting Virginia Lucas in a short lunchtime recital programme, in 'selected venues' with other members of the company.

The marketing director has, however, created an incipient revolution in the company, and has plainly been spreading gossip outside. This must be stopped. A company meeting must be told the economic truth about the autumn tour, a new marketing director appointed as soon as possible, and the marketing material revamped to take advantage of the 'new direction', and 'new spirit' in the company. The bookers should be rung with the reassuring news that rehearsals are going well, and that it is announced that the famous Virginia Lucas will appear, additionally, in a few lunchtime recital programmes in the tour venues.

10.7 Building the audience

Remembering that most people go for the first time (or come back after a long time) to the theatre in a group, the marketing should concentrate hard on group selling for the 'new' Civic. The programme must indeed be built around all segments of the community; if gardening, DIY and cookery are major interests in the area then the programme must include gardening talks, DIY demonstrations and cookery presentations. The marketing must then target a series of groups for each part of the programme. Everyone from the Townswomen's Guilds to the Young Farmers need to be 'sold' two or three shows, with attractive group concessionary rates.

The format of presentation on posters, throwaways and mailshots needs to be fresh and new. Advertising needs to be newly located in locations formerly neglected. Promotion needs to be targeted on visitors to the area's other amenities – parks, supermarkets, sports centres, clubs and hotels. There should be as many 'booking desks' as possible – in stations, garages, markets, car boot sales pitches. The newness and attractiveness of the season needs to be emphasized in every contact with the public, and the image should be 'humanized' by profiles of the new Libra staff, and items of 'Libra news' planted in local news media.

10.8 The amateur societies

a) The amateur operatic society

Calculation of likely costs per seat in the two venues will make it clear that the Corn Exchange Hall is not as attractive as it might appear. There is also the important point that many members will see moving as something of a deterioration in their standards if the society moves to a smaller venue without a pit. Sponsorship is a possibility, but a more dynamic approach would be (remembering that the largest part of the production costs can be spread over any number of performances) actually to increase the length of the run at the Grand Opera House. They were certainly well supported last year; the loss came from poor budgeting and a poor pricing policy rather than from lack of support. But is *Kismet* the right choice anyway?

b) The music society

A more adventurous programme must be 'sold' to likely local attenders; special meetings with local church organists, conductor(s) of local choirs, school music teachers and private instrumental teachers should promote and 'sell' it. The membership should then be enlarged (a better strategy than putting membership fees up) by offering concessions on membership at the door to new attenders. (Offer specially devised group concessions for each recital to targeted groups, so there are new attenders.) Offer promotional 'trial' memberships to students.

Encourage the committee to delegate fund raising to a special fund raising group. Their programme should ideally not be seen as an appendix to the main programme but as complementary to it, even, sometimes, a part of it. Short fund raising items such as auctions of musical memorabilia may occasionally be inserted at a suitable point in a programme, but more usually the fund raising events will be advertised at the concerts (and vice versa). Fund raising events should be worthwhile in themselves, and should include musical content, as in musical quiz games, or live music played at coffee mornings, garden parties or barbecues. In that way the society suffers no strain from having to change its nature while raising funds, and the programme is seen as a whole, not one half as 'vulgar but popular' and the other half 'serious but subsidized'.

10.9 The threat of the multiplex

There is no point in wasting time, money and effort opposing the building of the multi-screen cinema. It is better from the first to look for possible areas of cooperation with it when it comes. Yet it will obviously have a considerable impact, and that leaves two immediate possibilities. The first is to play on the strengths of having a characterful old theatre; in design and promotion play up its 'character', and diversify the programme accordingly, with some stage shows, 'themed' classic film series and perhaps a sequence of 'art' films. The second possibility is to investigate the costs of 'twinning' the interior, so that Georgina too may provide a choice of films (even showing four different films nightly). A further advantage of this would be that she could then obtain films that distributors will only hire out with a particular second film.

10.10 Having a good day

All these omens may together appear to be harbingers of doom, but they may be unrelated, and may not be bad news at all. The managing director must plainly make no moves until the facts are known, and must organize things so that this happens rapidly. The managing director needs to deal quickly with the knock on the door, then arrange, if possible, to have a secretary 'screening' callers. Assuming that could be arranged the best first call to make would probably be to Sir Humphrey. While explaining what is being done about Mr and Mrs Foljambe's letter, the managing director can make guarded enquiries about the other matters. According to the information gathered, a sequence of further calls should then suggest itself.

Appendix A Useful addresses

INTERNATIONAL BODIES

The British Council,
10 Spring Gardens,
London SW1A 2BN

Visiting Arts,
11 Portland Place,
London W1N 4EJ

European Forum for Arts and Heritage,
1 rue Defacqz,
1050 Brussels,
Belgium

British Incoming Tour Operators Association,
Vigilant House,
120 Wilton Road,
London SW1V 1JZ

NATIONAL BODIES

Department of National Heritage,
2–4 Cockspur Street,
London SW1Y 5DH

Arts Council of England,
14 Great Peter Street,
London SW1P 3NQ

Arts Council of Northern Ireland,
185 Stranmillis Road,
Belfast BT9 5DU

Arts Council of Scotland,
12 Manor Place,
Edinburgh EH3 7DD

Arts Council of Wales,
9 Museum Place,
Cardiff CF1 3NX

Museums and Galleries Commission,
16 Queen Anne's Gate,
London SW1H 9AA

The Council of Museums in Wales,
32 Park Place,
Cardiff CF1 3BA

Northern Ireland Museums Advisory Committee,
185 Stranmillis Road,
Belfast BT9 5DU

Scottish Museums Council,
County House,
20–22 Torphichen Street,
Edinburgh EH3 8JB

Crafts Council,
44A Pentonville Road,
Islington,
London N1 9BY

British Film Institute,
21 Stephen Street,
London W1P 1PL

Design Council,
28 Haymarket,
London SW1

Association for Business Sponsorship of the Arts,
Nutmeg House,
60 Gainsford Street,
Butler's Wharf,
London SE1 2NY

Royal Society of Arts,
8 John Adam Street,
London WC2N 6EZ

English Heritage,
Fortress House,
23 Saville Row,
London W1X 1AB

National Trust,
36 Queen Anne's Gate,
London SW1 9AS

Rural Development Commission,
11 Cowley Street,
London SW1 3NA

Charities Commission,
St Albans House,
57–70 Haymarket,
London SW1Y 4QX

BBC,
Broadcasting House,
Portland Place,
London W1

Independent Broadcasting Authority,
70 Brompton Road,
London SW3

Historic Buildings Councils, England,
25 Saville Row,
London W1

Historic Buildings Council, Scotland,
25 Drumsheugh Gardens,
Edinburgh EH3

Historic Buildings Council, Wales,
Welsh Office,
Cathays Park,
Cardiff

National Arts Collections Fund,
8 Duncannon Street,
London WC2

British Library,
2 Sheraton Street,
London W1

National Library for Scotland,
57 George IV Bridge,
Edinburgh EH1 1EW

National Library for Wales,
Llyfrgell Genedlaethol Cymru,
Aberystwyth SY23 3BU

British Tourist Authority,
Thames Tower,
Black's Road,
Hammersmith,
London W6 9EL

English Tourist Board,
Thames Tower,
Black's Road,
Hammersmith,
London W6 9EL

Northern Ireland Tourist Board,
St Anne's Court,
59 North Street,
Belfast BT1 1NB

Scottish Tourist Board,
23 Ravelston Terrace,
Edinburgh EH4 3EU

Welsh Tourist Board,
Brunel House,
2 Fitzalan Road,
Cardiff CF2 1UY

National Lottery Arts Board,
Arts Council of England,
14 Great Peter Street,
London SW1P 3VQ

National Lottery Sports Board,
Sports Council of England,
16 Upper Woburn Place,
London WC1H 0QP

National Heritage Memorial Fund,
10 St James's Street,
London SW1A 1EF

National Lotteries Charity Board,
St Vincent House,
30 Orange Street,
London WC2H 7HH

The Millennium Commission,
2 Little Smith Street,
London SW1P 3DH

NATIONAL ASSOCIATIONS

National Campaign for the Arts,
Francis House,
Francis Street,
London SW1P 1DE

SALVO – Scottish Arts Lobby,
c/o Royal Lyceum Theatre,
Grindlay Street,
Edinburgh EH3 9AX

Association of County Councils,
Eaton House,
66a Eaton Square,
London SW1W 9BH

Association of District Councils,
26 Chapter Street,
London SW1P 4ND

Association of Metropolitan Authorities,
35 Great Smith Street,
Westminster,
London SW1P 3BJ

Association of Leading Visitor Attractions,
25 King's Terrace,
London NW1 OJP

British Association of Leisure Parks, Piers and Attractions,
25 King's Terrace,
London NW1 OJP

Historic Houses Association,
2 Chester Street,
London SW1X 7BB

National Society of Painters,
Sculptors and Printmakers,
17 Carlton House Terrace,
London SW1

Dance UK,
9 Rossdale Road,
London SW15 1AD

ADAPT Trust (Access for Disabled People in Arts Premises Today),
Cameron House,
Abbey Park Place,
Dunfermline,
Fife KY12 9PZ

Association of Independent Museums,
Hotties Science and Arts Centre,
PO Box 68,
Chalon Way,
St Helens,
Merseyside WA9 1LL

Museums Association,
42 Clerkenwell Close,
London EC1R OPA

Incorporated Society of Musicians,
10 Stratford Place,
London W1N 9AE

Association of British Orchestras,
Francis House,
Francis Street,
London SW1P 1DE

Incorporated Society of Musicians,
10 Stratford Place,
London W1N 9AE

Public Art Commissions Agency,
Studio 6,
Victoria Works,
Victoria Street,
Birmingham B1 3PE

Public Art Development Trust,
1a Cobham Mews,
Agar Grove,
London NW1 9SB

Arts Development Association,
Room 110,
The Arts Centre,
Vane Terrace,
Darlington,
Co. Durham DL3 7AX

Book Trust,
Book House,
45 East Hill,
London SW18

Public Art Development Trust,
6–8 Rosebery Avenue,
London EC1R 4TD

Rural Enterprise Unit,
National Rural Enterprise Centre,
NAC,
Stoneleigh,
Warwickshire CV8 2LZ

British Arts Festivals Association,
PO Box 925,
London N6 5XX

Contemporary Arts Society,
Tate Gallery,
20 John Islip Street,
London SW1P 4LL

Voluntary Arts Network,
PO Box 1LE,
Newcastle upon Tyne NE99 1LE

NATIONAL UNIONS AND PROFESSIONAL ORGANIZATIONS

National Association of Theatrical, Television and Kine Employees,
155 Kennington Park Road,
London SE11 4JU

British Actors Equity Association,
8 Harley Street,
London W1N 2AB

Musicians Union,
29 Catherine Place,
London SW1

Writers Guild of Great Britain,
430 Edgware Road,
London W2 1EH

Institute of Leisure and Amenity Management,
Lower Basildon,
Reading,
Berkshire

Institute of Entertainment and Arts Management,
3 Trinity Road,
Scarborough YO11 2TD

Institute of Travel and Tourism,
113 Victoria Street,
St Albans,
Hertfordshire AL1 3TJ

Variety and Allied Entertainments Council of Great Britain,
403 Collingwood House,
Dolphin Square,
London SW1V 3NE

National Artists Association,
17 Shakespeare Terrace,
Sunderland SR2 7JG

Theatrical Management Association,
Bedford Chambers,
Covent Garden,
London WC2E 8HQ

Association of British Professional Conference Organizers,
54 Church Street,
Tisbury,
Salisbury,
Wiltshire SP3 6NH

Association of British Travel Agents,
55/57 Newman Street,
London W1P 4AH

Minority Arts Advisory Service,
26 Shacklewell Lane,
London E8

Institute of Charity Fundraising Managers,
1 Nine Elms Lane,
London SW8 5NQ

Performing Rights Society Ltd.,
29/33 Berners Street,
London W1P 4AA

REGIONAL ORGANIZATIONS

English Regional Arts Boards,
5 City Road,
Winchester,
Hampshire SO23 8SD

East Midlands Arts,
Mountfields House,
Forest Road,
Loughborough,
Leicestershire LE11 3HU

Eastern Arts,
Cherry Hinton Hall,
Cherry Hinton Lane,
Cambridge CB1 4DW

London Arts Board,
Elm House,
3rd Floor,
133 Long Acre,
London WC2E 9AF

North West Arts Board,
12 Harter Street,
Manchester M1 6HY

Northern Arts,
9–10 Osborne Terrace,
Jesmond,
Newcastle upon Tyne NE2 1NZ

South East Arts,
10 Mount Ephraim,
Tunbridge Wells,
Kent TN4 8AS

South West Arts,
Bradninch Place,
Gandy Street,
Exeter EX4 3LS

Southern Arts Board,
13 Clement Street,
Winchester,
Hampshire SO23 9DQ

West Midlands Arts,
82 Granville Street,
Birmingham B1 2LH

Yorkshire and Humberside Arts,
21 Bond Street,
Dewsbury,
West Yorkshire WF13 1AX

Committee of Area Museum Councils,
141 Cheltenham Road,
Cirencester,
Gloucester GL7 2JF

Area Museum Council for the South West,
Hestercombe House,
Cheddon Fitzpaine,
Taunton TA2 8LQ

Area Museums Service for South Eastern England,
Ferroners House,
Barbican,
London EC2Y 8AA

East Midlands Museums Service,
Courtyard Buildings,
Wollaton Park,
Nottingham NG8 2AE

North of England Museums Service,
House of Recovery,
Bath Lane,
Newcastle upon Tyne NE4 5SQ

North West Museums Service,
Griffin Lodge,
Cavendish Place,
Blackburn BB2 2PN

West Midlands Area Museum Service,
Hanbury Road,
Stoke Prior,
Bromsgrove,
Worcestershire B60 4AD

Yorkshire and Humberside Museums Council,
Farnley Hall,
Hall Lane,
Leeds LS12 5HA

Cumbria Tourist Board,
Ashleigh,
Holly Road,
Windermere,
Cumbria LA23 2AQ

East Anglia Tourist Board,
Toppesfield Hall,
Hadleigh,
Suffolk 1P7 5DN

East Midlands Tourist Board,
Exchequergate,
Lincoln,
Lincolnshire LN2 1PZ

Heart of England Tourist Board,
Woodside,
Larkhill Road,
Worcester,
Worcestershire WR5 2EF

North West Tourist Board,
Swan House,
Swan Meadow Road,
Wigan Pier,
Wigan,
Lancashire WN3 5BB

Northumbria Tourist Board,
Aykley Heads,
Durham,
County Durham DH1 5UX

South East England Tourist Board,
The Old Brew House,
Warwick Park,
Tunbridge Wells,
Kent TN2 5TU

Southern Tourist Board,
40 Chamberlayne Road,
Eastleigh,
Hampshire SO5 5JH

West Country Tourist Board,
60 St David's Hill,
Exeter,
Devon EX4 4SY

Yorkshire and Humberside Tourist Board,
312 Tadcaster Road,
York,
North Yorkshire YO2 2HF

Highlands and Islands Enterprise,
Bridge House,
20 Bridge Street,
Inverness IV1 1QR

Mid-Wales Tourism,
Canolfan Owain Glyndwr,
Machynlleth,
Powys SY20 8EE

North Wales Tourism,
77 Conway Road,
Colwyn Bay,
Clwyd LL29 7LN

Tourism South Wales,
Pembroke House,
Charter Court,
Phoenix Way,
Enterprise Park,
Swansea SA7 9DB

Appendix B The arts administrator's contacts

It is unfortunately true that experience suggests that plans and 'strategies' for the arts tend to cause rather more turbulence while they are being prepared than when they are finally published. However it may still be useful to have Challans, T. and Webber, H. (1993) *A Creative Future. The way forward for the arts, crafts and media in England* (HMSO) to hand. Certainly it is always important to have up-to-date information on available funding. Details of current government schemes are obtainable from the relevant arts councils and museum councils. Information on current European schemes may be obtained from the European Forum for Arts and Heritage. Useful funding directories are:

The Arts Funding Guide (Directory of Social Change)
Company Giving in Europe (Directory of Social Change)
The Central Government Grants Guide (Directory of Social Change)

There are a number of annual reference books for addresses and contacts, including:

The Performing Arts Year Book (Rhinegold)
The British Theatre Annual (Windmill Press)
Artists and their Agents (Windmill Press)
Who's Who in Art (Trade Press)
Writers and Artists Yearbook (A. and C. Black)

Other useful information and assistance may be obtained from:

PIN Targeting Service,
English Tourist Board,
Thames Tower,
Black's Road,
Hammersmith,
London W6 9EL

Code of Professional Conduct,
Chartered Society of Designers,
29 Bedford Square,
London WC1

Tax Benefits for the Arts,
Department of National Heritage,
2–4 Cockspur Street,
London SW1Y 5DH

Advisory, Conciliation and Arbitration Service (ACAS),
11–12 St James' Square,
London SW1

Appendix C Training for arts administration

Postgraduate Diploma in Arts Administration, MA in Arts Management, MA in Arts Management in Education, MA in Arts Criticism:
Department of Arts Policy and Management,
City University,
Frobisher Crescent,
Barbican,
London EC2Y 8HB

MA in European Cultural Policy and Administration:
Theatre Studies,
University of Warwick,
Coventry CV4 7AL

MA in Arts Administration:
Anglia Polytechnic University,
East Road,
Cambridge CB1 1PT

Postgraduate Diploma in Arts Management:
Arts Management Centre,
Faculty of Arts and Design,
Squires Building,
University of Northumbria at Newcastle,
NE1 8ST

HNC/HND Arts Management:
Fife College,
St Brycedale Avenue,
Kirkaldy KY1 1EX

Farnborough College of Technology,
Boundary Road,
Farnborough,
Hants GU14 6SB

Bournemouth and Poole College of Art and Design,
Wallisdown,
Poole,
Dorset BH12 5HH

Edinburgh's Telford College,
Crewe Toll,
Edinburgh EH4 2NZ

Undergraduate degree in Arts Administration:
De Montfort University,
Scraptoft,
Leicester LE7 9SU

Diploma in Arts Administration (non-graduate):
Faculty of Arts and Humanities,
Roehampton Institute,
Digby Stuart College,
Roehampton Lane,
London SW1 5PH

Short Course Programmes:
Arts Training South,
CCE,
University of Sussex,
Brighton BN1 9RG

Arts Management Training Initiative Scotland,
Moray House Institute,
Heriot-Watt University,
Chessels Land,
Holyrood Road,
Edinburgh EH8 8AQ

De Montfort University,
Scraptoft,
Leicester LE7 9SU

Centre for Arts Management,
University of Liverpool,
PO Box 147,
Liverpool L69 3BX

Kingsway College,
Holborn Centre for the Performing Arts,
Three Cups Yard,
Sandland Street,
London WC1R 4PZ

Warrington University College,
Warrington Collegiate Institute,
Padgate Campus,
Fearnhead,
Warrington WA2 0DB

Birkbeck College,
Centre for Extra Mural Studies, London University,
26 Russell Square,
London WC1B 5DQ

NVQs,
Arts and Entertainment Training Council,
Clyde House,
Clydegate,
Bradford BD5 0BQ

Index